FISHING FOR SUMMER FLOUNDER

FISHING FOR SUMMER FLOUNDER

Fluke Jigging from Shore, Boat, and Kayak

By John Skinner

©2016. FISHING FOR SUMMER FLOUNDER
Fluke Jigging from Shore, Boat, and Kayak

Printed And Distributed by On the Edge Communications Inc.

Printed in the United States of America

ON THE EDGE COMMUNICATIONS INC.
WADING RIVER, NY 11792

ISBN 978-0-9906914-1-9

Design and Layout: Stacey Kruk-Damiano
www.skgraphics.net

Cover Design : Tommy Corrigan

Other Books by the Author
STRIPER PURSUIT
FISHING THE BUCKTAIL
A SEASON ON THE EDGE

DEDICATION

Dedicated to my wife Kim. A keeper for sure.

ACKNOWLEDGMENTS

Thanks go out to my brother, Captain Bob Skinner, and his wife, Marie, for editing the manuscript. Bob's perspective as a fisherman with an editor's eye and Marie's vantage point as an avid reader of a wide range of subjects combine to provide valuable guidance. My daughter, Katie, went through the manuscript with an amazing eye for every little detail. I sleep well at night knowing a Princeton graduate has proofread my manuscript. Thanks to Mike Mapes for taking me out on his boat for the ocean fluking trip that contributed to Chapter 9. Finally, thanks to Zeno Hromin of *The Surfcasters Journal* for his selfless assistance and priceless advice with the publishing details required to make this book a reality.

TABLE OF CONTENTS

CHAPTERS

1. INTRODUCTION 1

2. RIGS AND JIGS 5

3 PRESENTATION, RODS, AND REELS.........................21

4. BEACHES 29

5 INLETS 41

6. BAY SHORELINES, FLATS, AND DOCKS 53

7. SHALLOW KAYAK APPROACHES 65

8. SOUND STRUCTURE STRATEGIES 81

9. BIG WATER IN AND OUT 95

10. DEEP OCEAN PARTY BOAT 109

11. DOORMAT PURSUIT 121

12. MAKING FLUKE BUCKTAILS.......................................129

13. PARTING ADVICE 141

CHAPTER 1
INTRODUCTION

Whether you call them fluke or flounder, they're challenging, fun to catch, and among the best eating fish that inhabit the waters along the East Coast and Gulf States. They are widespread and easily accessible in many areas and inhabit a diverse range of environments. Anglers in pursuit of these fish can be found wading shorelines, kayaking inshore waters, or fishing from boats in a few feet of water all the way out to deep ocean wrecks. Finding *fluke*, as I prefer to call them, involves understanding how they relate to bottom structure, currents, and bait availability. Getting them to eat is made easier by learning something about their behavior and being able to anticipate how they'll react to your offering and presentation.

Fluke will hit many different kinds of baits and lures presented in a variety of ways. We're going to eliminate a lot of that complication by using a basic jigging rig, as jig fishing has become the primary and most productive method of targeting these fish in many areas. In the next chapter we'll start by looking at the details of this rather simple bucktail rig that will see only minor modifications as we fish the wide range of environments in subsequent chapters. Although I'm not typically a fan of history lessons in fishing books, it's useful to understand why fluke fishing methods have changed so much over the years.

Prior to the 1990's, almost all anglers targeted fluke by dragging bait strips and live bait across the bottom on rather heavy boat rods. A favorite offering on the East Coast was a strip of squid tipped with a spearing, sandeel, or live killie. When I fished for fluke in the 1970s and 80s, every trip started with either buying or harvesting bait. There was no thought of fishing for them any other way. This was before the days of super thin braided fishing line, so it required several ounces of lead to keep this offering in the fluke's near-bottom strike zone because of the extra drag in the water created by the thicker monofilament line. The heavy sinker required a fairly heavy rod to handle the weight. The result was that we winched fluke from the bottom on tackle much better suited for larger quarry. Those heavier rods were tiring to jig with, and almost no one was concerned with jigging anyway, as most of the effort toward catching these fish involved obtaining the best bait and then dragging it on the bottom. It worked pretty well and anglers caught fluke, but it wasn't very exciting. Many of the fish were caught by rods left unattended in rod holders, and it was hard to perceive these fish as anything but bait-sucking brown blobs laying on the bottom.

These days if you ease into a group of boats fishing for fluke, you'll still see some anglers *deadsticking*, which is a phrase used to describe just holding onto the rod without imparting any action. Look around though and you'll also see something very different – anglers actively enticing fluke by jigging lures, in most cases, enhanced with artificial bait. If you watch carefully you're almost sure to observe that the jiggers are out-fishing the deadstickers, and those jiggers are having a lot more fun doing it as their tackle has been scaled down to match their small jigs. Of immense importance to shore and shallow water anglers, these relatively light-weight payloads are cast easily, so the shallows and shorelines are now fair game and prime territory for convenient and exciting fluke fishing.

Exciting – it's a word I don't think too many anglers would associate with the bait dragging and heavy-geared approach of decades ago. Having pursued these fish with light jigging tackle from the shore to the ocean depths, I can't think of a better word to describe this fishery. These are aggressive predators that challenge one's angling skills in the same ways as other gamefish, and even more so in some circumstances. You'll never stumble luckily into a fluke blitz or feeding frenzy. These fish are always hidden, and you need to figure them out. It's a skillful structure-based fishery, and a very satisfying one to master.

I've recorded and watched many hours of underwater video of fluke reacting to various real and artificial baits. Those videos paint a picture of a nasty predator, and give the angler valuable insight into how best to find and target these fish in terms of rigging and fishing technique. I'll share a few key insights here, but will refer to most of the underwater observations as we fish the different settings in later chapters. First, these fish strike baits violently and easily consume a 6-inch offering in a split second. Some fluke anglers think that they should react to a hit by giving the fish time to eat. In the hundreds of hits I've watched I have yet to see a fluke chew in a gradual fashion on even the largest strip bait. They engulf it with a burst of speed. With this observation it's probably easy to understand why I'll suggest setting the hook as soon as you feel weight on the end of your line. If you attempt a hookset and miss a fluke, it will come back. I've observed this without fail and have also watched how a hooked fish that managed to shake free immediately recaptured the bait. It's as if the fish gets annoyed by missing or losing its prey. When given a choice of a steadily gliding fresh piece of bait or a bouncing artificial jig, they will pursue the jig almost every time. An offering with motion is like a magnet to these fish. Readers with Internet access will not have to take my word for these observations because they can watch for themselves on this book's video support website.

I've written this book to stand on its own, independent of its companion website that provides extensive video support for each chapter. My goal is for a reader without Internet access to feel that the information given in these pages is complete and thorough without viewing the videos. However, for the vast majority of readers who have access to the Internet, the combination of what is written and the free video support that I've provided will be both enlightening and entertaining. For example, I'll describe how to jig fluke from the beach in great detail, but the ability for me to *show* you what I'm writing about and for you to *watch* how fish react to the technique is beyond what anyone can accomplish with the written word alone. You'll find little square barcodes, called *QR Codes*, placed strategically throughout this book. Scan one of these with a tablet or smartphone and it will take you to the video support for the part of the book you're reading. There are many free QR Code scanners available in your app store if your mobile device does not already have one. For people like me who prefer the bigger screen of a desktop or laptop computer, the book's companion website, FlounderBook.com, will present the videos organized by chapters.

As of publication, the video support was very extensive, but it will be a living document in that I'll extend and refine it as I acquire additional relevant video.

Millions of people live in close proximity to these fish that are called *fluke* in the Northeast and most of New Jersey, and *flounder* just about everyplace else. To add to the nomenclature confusion, they are also referred to as *Summer Flounder* along much of the East Coast. *Southern Flounder* and *Gulf Flounder* are closely related species in the Southeast and along the Gulf of Mexico. Summer Flounder, Southern Flounder, and Gulf Flounder are very similar looking predators that all have a mouth full of teeth. The populations actually mix along parts of the East Coast off the Carolinas. These fish differ in appearance and behavior from the *Winter Flounder* of the Northeast, which have small mouths, no teeth, and are not addressed in this book. To keep it simple I'll refer to the collection of predatory Summer, Southern, and Gulf Flounder as *fluke*. In acknowledgment of the many anglers who call these *flounder*, I'll refer to their range as *The Flounder Coast*.

Before we hit the water, we'll need to cover *The Three Rs* – rods, reels, and rigs. A nice aspect of jig fishing is that things can be kept rather simple, and the same gear can be used in multiple environments. Looking at strategies to fish the different settings is where it gets really interesting. It's also very important because if you're successful from shore, kayak, and boat, in big and small waters, then you're well-positioned to be productive under most sea and weather conditions. There's a lot to cover. Let's go.

CHAPTER 2
RIGS AND JIGS

We'll start with the rig itself and suggest an objective for presentation in the next chapter. The gear required to make that presentation in the various environments and conditions will follow from there. Whether I'm fishing in a foot of water or a hundred feet, the foundation for my terminal rig is the same. There's a bucktail jig on the bottom and a teaser, often called a dropper lure, about a foot above that. The rig is simple and easy to tie. Take a four-foot length of Fluorocarbon leader material and tie a loop at the bottom for the bucktail, and a dropper loop about a foot above that for the teaser. Terminate the other end with a small barrel swivel and you're done. The bucktail loop can be something like a surgeon's or perfection loop. The dropper loop should stand around four inches off the main line. A Palomar or Clinch Knot is fine for connecting the barrel swivel to the leader.

The bottom loop is pushed through the eye of the bucktail and then over the jig itself and pulled tight. When attaching a teaser hook to the dropper loop, I make a twist in the line after the first time I pass the loop over the hook, and then loop over it a second time. Using loops to make the connections allows for fast and easy jig and teaser changes without additional hardware or the need to cut and retie the leader. This rig is also a time-saver when a fish gets tangled in the net because you can easily remove items from the rig to facilitate the untangling. Do not scrimp on the quality of the barrel swivel that will be used to connect the terminal rig to the main line. These are small to begin with and the cheaper ones are prone to corrosion and will weaken and might break at the wrong time. Pay a few cents more for high quality swivels such as Tsunami Centro or SPRO.

Almost all of my fluke fishing is done with 20-pound-test Fluorocarbon leaders, although I'll go to 25-pound-test along abrasive jetties and in deeper water applications that require more weight and heavier tackle. I do not feel that fluke are line shy, so I don't think Fluorocarbon is necessary for its low visibility properties. I use it because it's more abrasion resistant than regular monofilament. This is important because the bucktail and dropper loops sometimes end up in the fluke's mouth, and their teeth can damage softer lines. I'm able to catch dozens of fish on the same Fluorocarbon leader without concern, although I'm in the habit of checking frequently for damage. I try to avoid using leader material heavier than 25-pound-test because this creates extra drag in the water and robs the jig of some of its action. The rig as I described tying it ends up with about thirty inches of line between the dropper loop and the barrel swivel. That may seem excessive, but it makes grabbing the leader to land a fish very convenient.

As we fish the different environments in later chapters, we'll focus frequently on the jig weight chosen for the particular conditions. Let's consider the bucktails themselves. Almost all of my fluking is done with some variation of a SPRO Prime bucktail. I start by mentioning the SPRO brand specifically because their Prime bucktails have been around a long time and are widely available. The narrow head shape on these bucktails reduces drag in the water and therefore can be fished near the bottom with slightly less weight. The position of the hook eye is very important. By eye, I mean the loop that the line is attached to. Suspend a standard bucktail from a strand of line and you'll likely see it tilt backwards. That's fine, and as intended for applications where you're casting and pulling the jig mostly horizontally through the water. Try the same thing with a SPRO Prime bucktail and note how it hangs level. This is because the hook eye is set farther back on the jig head. This level orientation is ideal for vertical jigging.

Note how the hook eye placement on these bucktails affects how they hang from the line. The bucktail on the right is a SPRO Prime.

Choosing a jig with a razor sharp hook of the appropriate size for fluke fishing is crucial for success, especially if you're fishing with children or novice anglers. Fluke are a superb target for children to fish for. It's daylight fishing, often in beautiful weather, for a fish that's relatively easy to reel in on tackle a child can handle. Cruise along a fleet of fluke boats and you're almost sure to see families getting in on the fun. It's hard to get kids to set a hook. If you fish with the proper size and style hook, the fish will almost hook themselves the first time they dive for the bottom. If you're fishing with children or novice anglers, this will make a big difference in your catch. The desire to have what I felt were the best hooks in my bucktails was the motivation for making my own. I go through step-by-step instructions on how to tie these bucktails in Chapter Twelve. If you don't want to tie your own, no problem, several manufacturers in addition to SPRO are now making excellent fluke bucktails. I'll mention a couple that I'm familiar with and can vouch for. The bucktail manufacturers probably won't be pleased with me saying this, but I see no reason to go overboard with different colors when purchasing bucktails. If I had nothing but white bucktails, I'd be just fine. One of the reasons I feel this way is that you can easily adjust the color of your offering by using different color trailers, which we'll get into later in the chapter. Proper bucktail selection and presentation is far more important than color.

S&S Rattletails are superb fluke bucktails. The "Rattletail" name comes from a small rattle attached to the hook. If I'm tipping the jig with a Berkley Gulp bait, I usually remove the rattle so that I can push my Gulp trailer farther up the hook shank. Rattle aside, I like these bucktails because the hair density is similar to that of the bucktails I tie, and they use high quality hooks of the appropriate size for fluke. They are also extremely well-made bucktails in that the hair stays on and the paint job is nearly indestructible. While I said I'm always happy with plain white bucktails, their jigs are realistic looking and I admit reaching for their sea robin pattern jig when the fluke are feeding on crabs. Jigging World, based in Northern New Jersey, makes similar style high quality bucktails in a wide range of colors. They make bucktails down to 3/8 of an ounce that can double as dropper lures.

When we get to deep water jigging, I'll mention using 3-ounce and heavier jigs. Among these will be Blue Frog Deep Divers. In some circumstances

SPRO bucktails from 1/2 to 8 ounces.

you'll need relatively heavy jigs to stay in the strike zone. The problem is that many of the jigs heavier than 2 ounces have hooks that are too big for fluke fishing. The Blue Frog Deep Divers are made for fluke fishing with weights up to 8 ounces that carry a hook that's the right size for fluke. The heavier SPRO jigs are also made with appropriately sized hooks for fluke when you take into account the size of those jigs and the stiffer rods required to handle those weights. Although not technically a bucktail, the Tsunami Facet Jig is another option on the heavier end of the jig spectrum. These 3.5- and 6-ounce swing hook jigs have squid skirts, very life-like action, and excellent hooks.

Blue Frog Deep Diver glow bucktails from 2 to 8 ounces.

Throughout this book I'll focus on bucktails for the main jig. The deer hair on a bucktail is hollow, and therefore provides some buoyancy. When the correct weight bucktail is chosen, the result is a very natural and deadly swimming action. You could substitute other lead head jig lures for the bucktail, but I'll caution that when I tried to fish plain jig heads instead of bucktails, side-by-side comparisons showed the bucktail out-catching by a large margin. It's why I mentioned liking the hair density on the S&S jigs. Very sparsely tied bucktails aren't much different than naked jig heads. A good bucktail has enough hair to present a larger profile and slow the jig's descent.

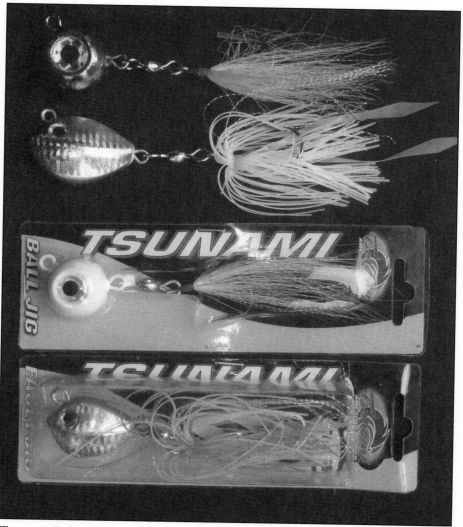

Tsunami Ball and Facet Jigs make excellent bucktail substitutes in deep water.

Bucktails are the most popular lures used for this fishing and are well-suited to carrying a variety of trailers. With few exceptions, the trailers on my fluke bucktails and teasers are some model of Berkley Gulp. For me and many other anglers, the introduction of Gulp revolutionized fluke fishing. Before Gulp, every fluke trip that I made was preceded by the need to purchase or harvest bait. Killies, sand eels, spearing, squid – I've fished them all, and with the exception of using an occasional strip of fresh fish for big fluke, I now tip my bucktails and teasers almost exclusively with Gulp.

My first bucket of Gulp sat in my boat for over a year without getting a chance. Then came the trip that changed my mind. I had an unusually full day of fluking planned. I would take my daughter and her friend out in the morning, then trade them for my son in the afternoon. The morning bite was ridiculous from the start, but we couldn't seem to break the 21-inch mark, which was the minimum size limit at the time. The kids caught fish at a pace that, between unhooking fish, cutting bait, and re-baiting jigs, it was impossible for me to fish. While in the middle of cutting up yet another squid, my eye caught the Gulp bucket. I figured this was a great time to see how well it worked, and if nothing else, it would partially relieve me of my cutting and jig baiting duties. The Gulp grubs worked, but I wasn't shocked given the aggressive nature of the fish. What did surprise me was that they pulled three keepers to the squid's zero. Also, I rarely had to replace a grub, as we could catch an impressive number of fish on each bait. The other real winner was that the fish couldn't steal it. Miss a hit? You can just leave it down because they rarely steal it. This meant no more bait checking and re-baiting of empty hooks each time a fluke stole the bait. It also struck me that the Gulp was over a year old, had sat through a lot of hot weather, but still caught very well.

After trading kids at a nearby beach, I decided my son and I would do a little experiment on the return trip. He would use only Gulp to tip his lures, and I would use only squid on mine. Fluke were flying over the side even faster on the afternoon session. When we passed 50 fish in slightly more than an hour, we decided to fish until we broke 100 and call it quits. After just over 2 1/2 hours of fishing, we reached our goal and headed for home. The final score was Gulp 62, squid 38. It was easy to see why. While I frequently lost bait or had to check my bait after a missed hit, my son could just keep his jig down until he hooked up. There was just no beating that. Three of four keepers on the afternoon trip were caught on the Gulp.

After that day, I started putting Gulp up against other baits, but there was no beating its productivity. By the end of that fluke season I was converted to Gulp and have never looked back. I wondered if the fluke were hitting the Gulp because it smelled and tasted like real food, or if it just looked good in the water. We took some along on a Scuba trip to do a little test. At a point in the dive when we were sure there were some porgies in the area, we dumped a handful of the grubs on the bottom and backed off a few feet. We had only seconds to wait as porgies came in and devoured the baits in less than ten seconds. They were clearly eating them, and some were even fighting over them. You can watch this on the video support for this chapter.

I was impressed even more when I shot underwater video of dragging a 6-inch Gulp Squido both on a floating jighead and plain hook. These baits have tentacles and are made to be jigged. I was forced to deadstick

Berkley Gulp has revolutionized fluke fishing for many anglers.

them while drifting because jigging the underwater inline camera would have made the video too bouncy. My first reaction of seeing the Squido being dragged through the water with no added action was that it did not look very enticing. Instead of the tentacles wiggling or undulating they just stayed in the slightly curled position. I was basically dragging a blob of Gulp through the water. It was fascinating to watch the fluke swim up to it, almost as though they were evaluating its scent, and then gobbling it right up. I had placed little plastic tubes over the hook points because I didn't want to hook the fish on the camera rig. This didn't matter, as the fish often held on and swallowed the bait, which I couldn't retrieve until I got them in the boat to ease the protected hook out. It was hard to draw any other conclusion than the fluke liked the smell and taste of the Gulp, because they ate it right up.

Gulp is a godsend for kayak fishing where space for bait is at a premium. It's even more so for a wading angler or a mobile surfcaster where carrying bait of any kind can be a hassle. A Ziploc bag of these baits stuffed in a pocket or surfbag along with a few bucktail rigs is now all that's required to target fluke. Gulp is also excellent in casting applications because it won't fly off the hook like some soft natural baits.

There are different types and packaging of Gulp. I prefer Berkley Gulp Alive, which is the product in juice-filled plastic buckets. Regular Berkley Gulp comes in resealable plastic bags, which also contain the juice attractant. Many of the Gulp bait models work great for fluke jigging, but my favorite is their Swimming Mullet, which can best be described as a curly tailed grub. I'll refer to these as "grubs" throughout much of this book. Berkley Gulp Alive Swimming Mullets come in 4- and 5-inch sizes. Much of my fishing is done with the 4-inch model. When I'm in an area with some bigger fish and I want a bait with a larger profile, I'll go up to the 5-inch. My favorite colors are chartreuse and white. Berkley makes a 6-inch Gulp Swimming Mullet and a similar 6-inch Gulp Grub, but these are available only in bags of three and four respectively. These big trailers are favorites among those targeting large fluke over deep structure. No matter how they're packaged, Gulp is very cost-effective because you can catch several fish on each bait, and fish rarely steal it. I average over five fluke per Gulp Swimming Mullet. As long as the tail isn't torn off, I simply keep

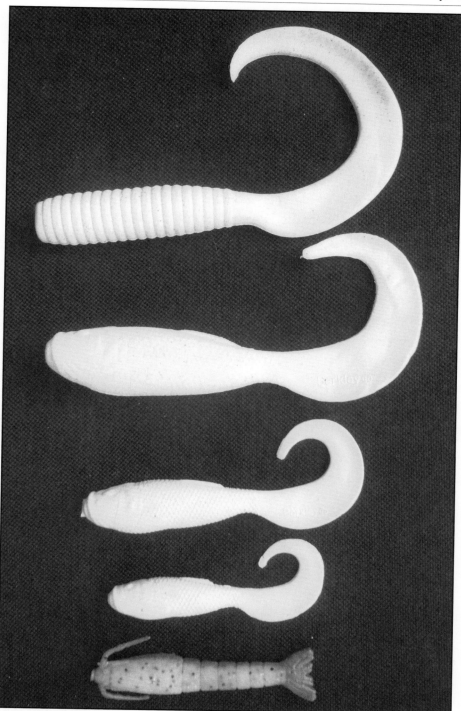

Gulp baits top to bottom – 6-inch Grub, 6, 5, and 4-inch Swimming Mullets, 3-inch Shrimp.

sticking them back on the hooks. I don't care whether the tail is up, down, or sideways. It's the flutter that counts. With this in mind, be aware that if the hair on your jig is rather long, it may interfere with that flutter. I trim the hair on any jig on which the grub tail doesn't flutter because of excessive hair length. After the Swimming Mullets, my next favorite is the 3-inch Gulp Alive Shrimp, New Penny color. These are deadly when the fish are feeding on crabs and shrimp. I've also caught well on the 6-inch Squido and 7-inch Jerk Shad.

Gulp is not the only choice when it comes to highly effective artificial baits. *Fishbites* are very popular among some anglers and offer a variety of bait models that work well on fluke. Their shrimp, paddle tail, and jerk bait products are all suitable for tipping your lures, and they catch and hold up well to multiple fish. Another excellent artificial bait manufacturer is Connecticut-based Otter Lures (otterlures.com). Their scented rippled bait strips come in several sizes. They're durable, have great action, and catch extremely well.

Fishbites are another artificial bait option for fluke anglers.

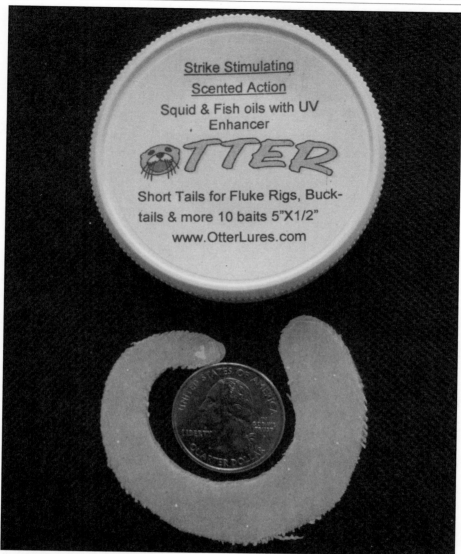

The rippled Otter Tails have an enticing swimming action.

When doing the kind of fluke jigging described in this book, a lot of the fish will be caught on the teaser lure. There's a wide range of offerings that make suitable droppers on a fluke rig. I'll cover some favorites here, but there's a lot of fun to be had experimenting with this part of the rig. If I could have only one teaser for fluke fishing, it would be a 3/8-ounce Tsunami Glass Minnow. This teaser is deadly when rigged with a 4-inch Swimming Mullet. It has very little drag in the water, and we'll see how this is a consideration in later chapters when we discuss line angle scoping. My next favorite teaser is a Tsunami Holo Teaser skirt over a 3/0 Gamakatsu Baitholder hook. This squid-like addition to a plain hook presents a bulkier profile and lots of flash. It's an attention getter that holds up very well to multiple fish. An important feature of both the Glass Minnow and Holo Teaser is that neither interferes with the undulation of the Gulp grub tail.

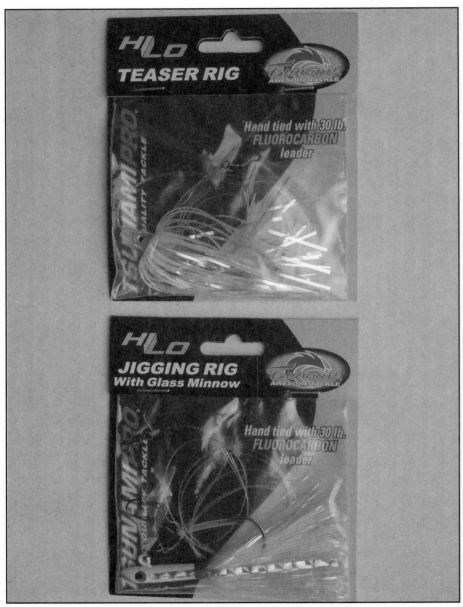

Tsunami offers pre-tied jigging rigs with their most popular fluke teasers.

I mentioned the Holo Teaser being an "attention getter". I think a lot about the importance of getting the attention of fluke when I choose colors, and my thoughts are influenced by my experience with underwater video. I've recorded fluke reacting to many different offerings, including live killies on a plain hook. Although fluke happily gobbled up the live killies once they saw them, the killies on a bare hook attracted far fewer fluke than any other offering. This made me realize that catching the attention of fluke was at least as important as offering them something enticing. With this in mind, I often have some chartreuse on my rig, whether that be a Gulp bait or a bucktail. I commonly use a chartreuse grub on the bucktail and a New Penny shrimp on the teaser hook. I feel the bright color can be seen easily and will bring the fluke close, and then they'll have a choice of striking that or the more natural looking shrimp. White is also a good choice as it's a natural color that is seen easily underwater.

When wading or shore casting I'll often use just a plain 3/0 Gamakatsu Baitholder hook tipped with a Gulp bait as the teaser. In these shore-bound applications the addition of a separate teaser lure can add wind resistance on the cast and cut into casting distance. With or without a skirt, the hook choice is very important. I go with the 3/0 Gamakatsu Baitholder because it is strong, the right size, and super sharp. The bait holder barbs on the shank help keep the Gulp bait in place, and that shank has the right length for the Gulp. Another positive feature of the shank length is that it is long enough to make unhooking fish easier without requiring the use of pliers. Sometimes it's unavoidable, but I try not to use pliers on my fluke bucktails and teaser hooks because it's too easy to damage the point or barb. Gamakatsu Octopus hooks are effective for catching fluke with Gulp baits, but their shorter shanks make these hooks harder to remove from a fish without pliers or tearing up your fingers.

The rig I've described won't do you much good without the correct presentation. While the angler is responsible for imparting the action on the rig that will attract and trigger the fish, proper execution is difficult without the appropriate rod and reel. We'll simplify this in the next chapter and then move on to the fishing.

CHAPTER 3

PRESENTATION, RODS, AND REELS

For vertical jigging from a boat or kayak, the objective is to bounce the rig rapidly while it glides a foot or two off the bottom with the drift of the boat. When casting, a slow retrieve is combined with the rapid jigging action in that near-bottom strike zone. Here is one of the most important tips in this book: You want to do this with the lightest weight jig possible that allows you to stay in the strike zone. If your jig is not heavy enough when vertical jigging, you'll need to keep letting line out to stay near the bottom. This is often referred to as *scoping*, and will continually increase the angle of your line. You want to avoid this and instead use a bucktail with a weight that will let you fish almost straight down, or on a slight angle out. If you fish with a bucktail that's too heavy, your line will be straight down as desired, but the jig will have very unnatural action as it seeks out the bottom like a rock. Somewhere between too heavy and too light is the proper weight jig that will glide, dart, and swim in a realistic fashion. When casting, a jig that's not heavy enough will swim too high off the bottom on the retrieve. A jig that's too heavy will drag the bottom ineffectively. If you're a novice angler, just keep this objective in mind for now, as we'll address it again in the upcoming chapters.

As mentioned in the introduction, set the hook immediately and hard when you feel weight on the line. The underwater videos show repeatedly how a fluke will hit again if you miss it. A nice benefit of the fast hookset is that it is very rare to gut hook a fish, as is often a problem when dragging baits and deadsticking. This is very important because it's often necessary to cull through a significant number of undersized fluke for every one that's large enough to keep legally. We want those released fish going back in the water in the best condition possible.

I normally avoid writing that you must do something a certain way, but I'll make an exception here for fishing line – you should be fishing with a modern-day braided superline. These lines generally consist of braided strands of Spectra or Micro-dyneema and have been referred to as *superlines* for decades to help differentiate them from braided Dacron and some older braided lines that predate monofilament. I'm referring to braided lines with product names such as Spiderwire and Power Pro. The superlines have a very high strength to diameter ratio. The 15-pound-test braid that I'll use in much of the fishing in this book has the same diameter as 4-pound-test monofilament line. This smaller diameter translates to much less drag in the water, which in turn allows for the use of light-weight jigs. Braided lines also have very little stretch. If you've watched some of the underwater support video, you will have seen how intensely fluke are drawn to a lively bouncing jig and teaser combination. If you try to impart this action with monofilament line, the stretch will absorb much of the energy of your jigging efforts. Instead of bouncing the jig, you'll just be exercising the stretch in the line as if it were a rubber band. That low stretch property of braided line also provides very high sensitivity. With braid, you feel everything because the activity is so efficiently transmitted to your rod. This also allows for rock-solid hooksets. Be sure to keep the line tight

 when spooling a reel with braid. If the braid is spooled loosely it can dig into itself when pressure is applied. A Palomar knot is a good choice for joining the braided main line to the barrel swivel of the terminal rig.

I prefer light conventional, or baitcasting, tackle for vertical jigging from boat and kayak, and spinning gear for all casting. The baitcasting tackle allows for more convenient depth control when fishing vertically. The use of spinning gear for casting is a personal preference, but one that I share with most anglers in my region

In the vertical jigging applications of boat and kayak, the main requirements of the rod are to put lively action on the jig, set the hook firmly, and fight the fish. If we solve the first requirement, the others will follow. The first consideration when choosing a vertical jigging rod is to make sure the tip of the rod is firm enough to impart that lively bouncing. If you choose a rod that's too soft for the jigs you are using, the rod will absorb the energy of the action that you're imparting. While you might be jigging aggressively, the jig won't be doing much because the soft rod will dampen the action.

I'll mention some specific rod models as reference points and examples, but there are many fine choices from a long list of manufacturers that will do the job. I'll stick to 7-foot rods because they're a good all-around choice for the various environments that we'll fish in the upcoming chapters. When choosing rods, I usually don't read too much into the manufacturer lure weight ratings. Different manufacturers arrive at these in different ways, so they're only approximate guidelines at best. Let's start with the baitcasting outfits. I'll use a Tsunami Classic Series TSCC701MH, rated 10- to 20-pound-test line for jigs up to 1 1/2 ounces. Their TSCC701H, rated for 12- to 25-pound-test line is good in the 1- to 3-ounce range. I fish 15-pound-test braided line on both of these rods. The TSCC701XH, rated 15- to 30-pound test line is good in the 3- to 6-ounce range, but can handle heavier jigs in a pinch. I move up to 20-pound-test braid on this stiffer rod. If a half-pound or more of lead is required to stay down, then we're getting out of the range where this relatively light tackle vertical jigging is going to be comfortable. We'll get to this in Chapter Ten.

If your rod is capable of putting good action on your jig, then it will be effective at setting the hook and should have no trouble bringing a large fluke to the surface, given a reel with a properly set and smooth drag. I do have brand preferences for reels because I'm looking for models with a flipping switch, and for reasons I don't understand, this is an uncommon feature. Many baitcasting reels have a thumb bar that you can press to disengage the clutch and let line out. Almost all of these reels require that you make a partial turn of the reel handle to re-engage the clutch to stop the line from going out. A flipping switch allows you to operate the reel in a mode in which the clutch will re-engage when you release the pressure on the thumb bar. Because there's no need to turn the handle, you're afforded very easy one-handed depth control. At the time of this writing, the Quantum Accurist PT AC100 was one of very few reels with this feature. Note that this reel usually ships with the flipping switch turned off. You need to set the switch to the "Flip" position in order for the thumb bar to control the clutch as I've described. In late 2015, Abu Garcia released their Silver Max SM3 with a similar feature called a Rocket Clutch. This differs from the functionality of a flipping switch in that releasing pressure on the thumb bar won't re-engage the clutch, but pushing a button right next to it will. This gives the angler the same kind of one-handed depth control as a flipping switch.

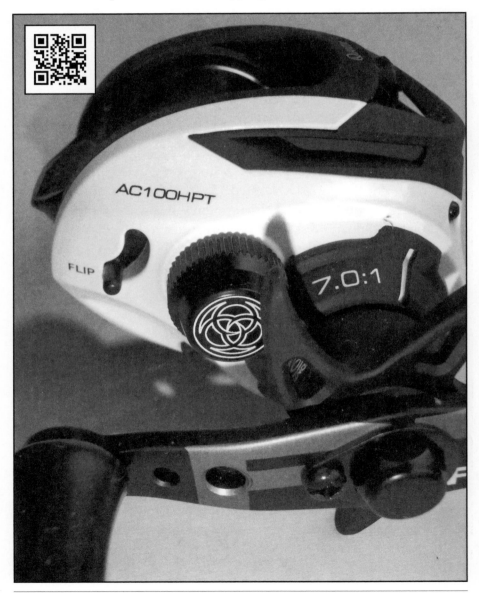

Garcia Silver Max 3 (top) and Quantum Accurist (bottom).

While the Accurist and Silver Max are fine inshore and shallow water reels, anglers who spend most of their time bouncing 3-ounce and heavier jigs in deep water will probably want something with a little more cranking power. Although there are many small conventional

The Maxel 20 Hybrid is a lightweight but heavy duty option for deep water applications.

reels on the market that are suitable for this fishing, it's important to avoid adding so much weight to the rod that vigorous jigging becomes uncomfortable. One excellent solution is the Maxel Hybrid 20. With stainless steel gears and 28 pounds max drag, the reel is well-suited for for much stronger gamefish than fluke, but weighs only 13 ounces. It even has a thumb bar, which is a feature that many anglers appreciate but is rare on this class of reel.

The 20 fish in 18 minutes video on this book's support website demonstrates the effectiveness of combining the tackle and technique advice given in this and the previous chapter. During the 18 minutes of that single drift, I attempt to set the hook 22 times, hook 21 fish, and land 20 of them. This very high conversion rate is due in part to proper rod selection. The rod is sensitive enough to detect the often subtle feeling of weight while jigging, but has a firm enough tip to put lively action on the rig and enough backbone to bury the hook. The other key to converting a high percentage of hits to landed fish is proper timing with respect to setting the hook. I'm keyed on that feeling of extra weight while bouncing the jig, and when I feel it, I set hard. Because the hooks on my rig are an appropriate size, style, and are razor sharp, they penetrate and hold easily. The effectiveness of the rapid jigging action also stands out on this drift. With a slight breeze blowing in opposition to the current, the drift speed was very slow, reading only in the 0.4- to 0.5-mph range on my GPS. We'll address drift speeds more in later chapters, but anyone who has ever dragged strip baits across the bottom slowly in the presence of crabs knows what the result is. With the proper gear to maintain lively action on the rig, I avoided the crabs while attracting and triggering many fluke.

It's also worth mentioning that the same two Gulp Swimming Mullet baits were used through that drift. Part of the credit goes to the design of the Tsunami Glass Minnow teaser. It has a very sharp hook of the proper size with just the right shank length to keep the grub from being pulled back. Out of the 20 fish landed on that drift, 15 fell to the teaser without changing the Gulp grub. That same piece of Gulp continued to produce on the next drift as well. It's hard to find a more cost-effective delivery tool for a Gulp Swimming Mullet.

The spinning tackle that I prefer for fluke casting has to cast the rig well in addition to the requirements mentioned for baitcasting tackle. While some anglers will occasionally cast for fluke in deep water, all of the casting that we'll do in upcoming chapters will be in shallow environments where the jig weights will range from 1/2 to 1 1/2 ounces. Given the narrow weight range, you could get by with a single medium action spinning rod for all of this fishing. A Penn Battalion 7-foot spinning rod rated for 10- to 17-pound-test line with a Penn Clash 4000 reel is an example outfit. Any of the lower-priced 4000 series Penn reels would also be a good choice. There are endless other comparable combinations on the market from many manufacturers.

 While one rod could do it, I usually fish a slightly lighter Battalion rated for 8- to 15-pound-test line with a Clash 3000 on the ocean beach where I rarely fish jigs heavier than 3/4 of an ounce. Let's go there and see why.

CHAPTER 4
BEACHES

I had my pick of parking spaces as my Jeep rolled into the barrier island parking lot a little after sunrise. With no preparation beyond grabbing my rod, surf bag, and a small cooler bag, I was on my way to the ocean's edge in just a few seconds. As the pavement transitioned to sand, I strained my eyes through the early morning light to read the barely perceptible bulges of water that confirmed what my ears told me when I first stepped out of the truck – the ocean was nearly flat on the immediate stretch of beach. This wasn't totally unexpected. Before I left the house, the online buoy readings indicated a gentle two-foot swell from the southeast. Because the beach closest to the parking lot also adjoined an inlet jetty that protruded 200 yards south into the ocean, the rocks were intercepting the small waves before they could reach the shore. As I looked to my right, in the opposite direction of the jetty, I noted significant whitewater where waves broke on the beach beginning a couple of hundred yards away. The slightly rougher water extended to a distant point that curved gradually into the ocean before turning back and hiding the rest of the shoreline from my view.

Given an incoming current reaching around the jetty and pouring into the inlet, the flat water in front of me was worth a few casts because it was easy to imagine baitfish and predators being pushed into the pocket formed by the intersection of the jetty and the beach. Several casts of the bucktail rig yielded nothing, and my eyes did no better in their search for baitfish. The lack of diving gulls or terns only reinforced my feeling that this spot was unlikely to produce. I was careful not to waste any time here, as I was excited by the potential that existed farther down the beach.

The lack of baitfish wasn't necessarily a problem. If anything, their absence had the potential to make my job easier. I was confident there were fluke in the general area, and like any predator, they could almost certainly be counted on to be where the food was. Fluke frequently follow bait schools, such as sandeels, but they seem equally satisfied to feed on less mobile crustaceans, such as small crabs and shrimp. Mole crabs, also called sand fleas, were almost sure to be present. While these tasty morsels might not be able to move as fast as baitfish, their ability to bury themselves in the sand to evade predators is no less effective as a self-preservation technique. This is especially true in very calm water, but add churning wave action to scour away the protective sand and momentarily suspend the creatures in the water, and the odds begin tilting in the predators' favor. This is exactly what I envisioned happening several hundred yards down the shoreline where the bigger waves chewed at the beach. My excitement at this scenario came from the realization that the food source would not only be concentrated in the turbulence where waves broke on the beach, it would also be very easy to reach with even the lightest weight jigs.

The main factors involved in choosing the jig weight are water depth and movement. I estimated that the deepest water that I could cast to with light tackle in this area would be about six feet deep. There was little water movement generated by tidal current, and very little lateral movement generated by the small waves. I rigged accordingly with a 3/4-ounce bucktail tipped with a 4-inch white Berkley Gulp Alive Swimming Mullet. I chose a 3-inch Gulp Alive Shrimp in New Penny color on a plain 3/0 hook for the dropper lure. The Gulp Shrimp is almost always my first choice on the dropper hook when I expect fluke to be feeding on crustaceans. A 7-foot Penn spinning rod rated for 8- to 15-pound-test line matched with a Penn Conflict 3000 spooled with 15-pound-test braid was a good match for the payload, conditions, and fish.

I started heading for the white water, but stopped to make a cast every hundred feet or so as I moved along. Around twenty minutes into my effort and 300 yards down the beach, I set the hook on a firm grab, but was slightly disappointed when I felt the unmistakably characteristic rod pumps that indicated this was a sea robin rather than my intended target. It grunted as I pulled it onto the sand, and I was

A 3-inch Gulp Shrimp followed by a 4-inch Gulp Swimming Mullet on a 3/4-ounce S&S Rattletail bucktail.

careful of its sharp spines and armor plated spiked head as I grasped it with the towel rag that I had tucked into the back of my belt exactly for this purpose. While this wasn't the fish I wanted, I interpreted it as a step in the right direction and an encouraging sign. Fluke and sea robins are often mixed on the same grounds. I felt even more encouraged as I stepped into the wash to release it and noticed several sand fleas exposed momentarily in a receding wave. I moved about fifty feet down the beach before making my next cast.

Getting past sea robins is often a challenge for fluke anglers in many areas.

The first distinct taps of a flatfish were felt crisply against the background of my rapid jigging motion as my jig closed in on the last wave before the little shore break. As if I was ignoring the fish, I kept jigging until I felt weight and then quickly buried the hook with a sharp sweep of the rod skyward. The rod bent, but not much as I pulled the fish with the help of an approaching wave. I cranked quickly to assure that I wouldn't give it any slack and the opportunity to spit the jig. In a few seconds I had my first flatfish of the morning. As a 15-incher at a time when the minimum size limit was 18 inches, this fish was safe from the frying pan.

The fish hit in a special part of the surf often referred to as the *beach lip*. This is a shallow trough of water cut along the edge of the beach by wave action. If you've walked into the ocean and then suddenly stepped off a little ledge into deeper water, then you've experienced this important structure. Even though this trough is only about two feet deep, it's enough for gamefish to swim along while ambushing prey that have been disoriented by wave turbulence.

Whereas I was covering shoreline quickly before catching the sea robin, I was now changing to a mode where I would try to paint the shoreline in an attempt to find where the fluke were most concentrated. Now I would move only a few yards between casts, and maybe not at all when I caught one. While it might be tempting to stay put when I first started hooking up, experience had taught me that it was much better to keep moving. Fluke behavior was directly responsible for this approach.

Compared to gamefish such as striped bass, bluefish, sea trout, redfish, etc., fluke do not move much. If I was on this same stretch of beach and fishing for stripers, I could have some confidence that the bass would be running the shoreline and covering some ground as they searched for food. Fluke, on the other hand, are much more likely to stay put, often partially burying themselves and waiting to ambush their food. Even if not in this camouflaged ambush feeding mode, they're still not likely to cover ground with the speed of most other gamefish. Because they usually don't move much, it's often in the fluke angler's best interest to keep moving. Observe a fleet of boats fluke fishing and it's likely that every single one will be drifting in an attempt to intercept the fish. The beach angler is no more likely to maximize his catch by standing still as a boat angler would be by anchoring.

The farther I moved down the beach, the better the fishing got until it seem to stabilize at a hookup every two or three casts. Most were fluke, but the seemingly omnipresent sea robins mixed in. With the good bite I was now moving only a few feet between casts, but I was still moving. I drew a few lines in the sand by dragging my foot up the beach high enough that the rising tide wouldn't wash these fish marks away. As I approached the point that was nearly three quarters of a mile from where I started, the water became rougher, shallower, and the fishing slowed. It was time to turn around and double back. Instead of fishing all the way on the return, I walked directly to the last line that I had drawn in the sand. The first cast there produced a fluke that was only slightly short. A few casts and yards beyond that, I put my first keeper of the trip into my small cooler bag that was draped over my shoulder next to my surf bag. I marked this spot and decided I would focus and fish back and forth along a roughly hundred-foot stretch of beach that clearly held a good concentration of slightly larger fluke. At least I thought they were only slightly larger.

Even though most of the fluke were being caught within thirty feet of the shore, I was still casting as far as I could. With the light spinning rod, and the 3/4-ounce bucktail responsible for dragging two Gulp baits through the air into a breeze, my longest casts still weren't going very far. This particular cast was like all the rest. When it touched down less than a hundred feet from shore, I watched the line carefully as the jig sank until a slight twitch indicated it had hit bottom. I immediately yanked the rig off the bottom and began a rapid jigging action while I turned the reel handle slowly. My goal was to keep it twitching along just off the bottom. I dropped the angle of the rod lower to the water as the rig approached the last wave and beach lip. My hook-setting reflex kicked in hard on a sharp grab. The rod barely budged initially, then slowly eased as a wave came up behind the fish. I pulled and cranked hard as the fish bounced on top of the wave not unlike the big ones do on the deck of a boat. I was careful to keep the rod bent and not give any slack. As the wave receded the big fluke drummed the wet sand until the next wave helped me move it farther up the beach slope. My hand barely fit around its head as I grabbed it

This big fluke hit just behind the turbulence at the water's edge.

to carry it up the shore. Weighed a few hours later it pushed the scale to 7.8 pounds. A good fluke in any circumstance, but an exceptional one only a few feet from the beach and in less than three feet of water. My only regret was that it hit so close that I missed out on having it take a couple of runs that I'm sure it was capable of. From the time it hit until the time it was laying on the sand, video replay showed that only nine seconds had passed.

A successful ocean surf fluke trip usually depends on choosing a day when the waves hitting the beach are less than three feet. My trips start by surveying local weather buoys and webcams to check wave height, period, and direction. If I see onshore wave heights of two feet or less, I consider these good conditions. Onshore waves between two and three feet usually make for more challenging conditions, and downright difficult ones if they are long-period powerful waves such as those generated by an offshore storm. If the onshore ocean waves are higher than three feet, then I'll only fish the open ocean beach in an area where those waves are being cut down by a nearshore sandbar. If large waves are dissipating on a bar and then spilling into a trough area that borders the beach, this has the potential to hold easily fishable fluke that are taking advantage of food being dislodged from the bar in the same way that waves breaking on the beach will often attract fish along the beach lip. As with most kinds of fishing, some local knowledge of beach structure can go a long way toward planning and executing a successful trip.

Keep in mind that, as was the case on this trip, wave characteristics often vary as you move along the beach and encounter different beach structure. Success on this trip depended on finding the right water conditions. The water nearest the jetty this particular day was nearly flat and lacked the turbulence required to dislodge the small crabs that the fluke were feeding on. After I moved far enough down the beach to escape the calming influence of the jetty, I had enough wave action to expose this forage, but not so much that it was hard to work the jig. This was the hot spot. As I approached a significant point, the waves built and broke across a shallow bar that made white water that was better suited to striped bass than fluke.

When I was on this same beach a few days earlier, the ocean was rougher and the best fishing took place closer to the jetty. Whereas three-foot and higher waves crashed along most of the beach that day, the semi-protected area closer to the jetty provided those nice two-foot waves that stir things up a bit, but not too much. On some very calm days I often find the best fishing in the roughest water, but "rough" is a relative term in that situation, and may refer to small gentle waves. As an experienced striped bass surfcaster, I've found that I've needed to redefine what I consider "good water" when targeting fluke. Stripers like the nasty rough stuff, whereas my best shore-based fluke fishing is done in relatively calm surf with just enough turbulence to expose the various creatures that fluke feed on.

Finding the best spots to target fluke often involves reading the beach structure. I generally try to avoid flat and shallow structure, and instead seek out areas where the beach has a moderate to steep slope. When reading the beach, it's important to realize that the slope of the beach that you see often extends beneath the water. So a gently-sloped beach usually borders shallow water, whereas the steep beach usually indicates somewhat deeper water. Points on a beach frequently offer an angler a range of depths as you move across the point. It's typical that the side of the point that faces into the prevailing direction that waves come from can be scoured out, while the point itself is shallow. Move around the point and you might find a bowl of deeper water. When I'm fishing point structure, whether it be for fluke or stripers, I resist stopping on the first spot that produces fish. If fishing space permits, I'll work my way around the point in an effort to find the slice of structure where the fish are concentrated. Fluke love edges, so sandbars and cuts in sandbars are features that also deserve an angler's attention.

Keep in mind that the structure of some beaches can change drastically with storms, or in the case of many Northeast beaches after Hurricane Sandy, beach replenishment projects. It can be frustrating to have a good thing going and all figured out and then have the productive structure erased. With time, beaches will reshape themselves. This is especially true near inlets where regular currents do a good job of restoring prominent beach features.

The fish were very close to shore on this chapter's trip, but that's not always the case. Sometimes the water near the beach is shallow and a longer cast is required to hit sufficient depth. Other times the fluke might be set up on bait schools a little way off the beach. I can offer two solutions when casting distance is an issue. My first would be to remove the dropper hook, and fish with only the Gulp-tipped bucktail. The dropper often catches the bulk of the fish when I'm casting, but the air resistance it causes on the cast cuts significantly into casting distance. While it may seem that removing the dropper will reduce your catch severely, this is not necessarily true. While fish often hit the dropper in favor of the bucktail, those same fish are very likely to hit a properly presented bucktail if that's the only potential meal they get to look at. While it may be tempting, I would recommend against increasing the bucktail weight to increase distance. A bucktail that is too heavy for a given application does not swim naturally and will usually produce poorly. A second solution would be to leave the dropper on and replace the bucktail with something more aerodynamic, such as a small metal lure. In this case I would consider the metal lure, or tin, to function primarily as a delivery tool to get the dropper out to the fish. As opposed to the rapid jigging technique I suggest for bucktails, the tin should be fished on a slow retrieve with frequent twitches to catch the attention of and trigger fluke.

If you're accustomed to fishing vertically for fluke from a boat or kayak, you'll need to make some adjustments for casting. Fluke hit and fight much differently when casting for them and retrieving parallel to the bottom as opposed to vertical fishing from a boat. When casting, a hit often presents as slack line because the fish has grabbed your jig and kept its forward motion. If you feel slack, set the hook immediately! When you hook a fluke from above in a boat, it fights hard as it struggles to get back to the bottom. When casting you're simply pulling it at you, and it may glide the whole time and not feel like much. If you watch the underwater fluke videos that support this book, you'll see many instances of the fish engulfing an offering and then moving with the drift of the boat without giving any indication on the surface that there's a fish on the line. It's very important to crank down hard and maintain pressure on the fish so that it doesn't spit the hook, which is also observed several times on the supporting videos. This is especially important when fishing larger bodies of water where a hooked fish can be pushed at you by wave action. It's important to keep the pressure on, but be ready with a properly set drag because they have a habit of taking off hard once pulled into the shallows.

The biggest mystery to me concerning open beach fluke fishing is why I don't see more people doing it. The fish are frequently there in good numbers, drawn to the beach and bar turbulence that often chums the water with plenty of food. While smaller fish have a tendency to dominate the catch, there are often enough legal-sized fish to provide a fresh meal, and an occasional large flattie to make it even more interesting. What appeals to me most about this kind of fishing is the convenience. There's no dealing with boat or kayak launching and retrieval, and the necessary gear is minimal. A light spinning outfit, a couple of pre-tied rigs, and a Ziploc bag of Gulp is about all you'll need to get in on the fishing. Even if you have only an hour to spend at the shore, you can spend almost all of that hour fishing. For those on a tight budget, it couldn't be more cost-effective. This puts the fishery within reach of anyone who can access the thousands of miles of open water shoreline that borders the Flounder Coast. If you've never beach fished for fluke before, and you're not sure where to start, think about areas where boat anglers target fluke. The way I like to think about it is if I can stand on the beach and see boats fluke fishing, even a mile off the beach, then there are probably fish available within casting distance. Anglers often tell me of incidental fluke catches on the beach while fishing for other species. Any beach where anglers catch fluke accidentally is a great place to target them! While not all beaches will be productive, it's a good bet that the ones near inlets will offer shots at these fish as they move in and out of the protected waters that we'll discuss in upcoming chapters. Let's move on to an inlet.

CHAPTER 5
INLETS

I didn't like what I was seeing as I read the weather buoy data. The wind was sustained onshore at twenty knots with some higher gusts, and the seas were four feet. Fishing the open beach was out of the question. While casting into the stiff wind was marginally feasible given that I expected fish close to the beach, doing that with waves that were averaging four feet scuttled any thoughts of fishing the sand. The kayak was a definite option, not on the ocean, but on the sheltered bay behind the barrier island. There were problems with this choice too. Dealing with twenty-knot winds while drift-fishing in a kayak is difficult at best. Although the wind-driven drift could probably be reduced to a productive speed using a drift-control sock, paddling back into the wind at the end of every drift would be tiresome and chew up too much fishing time. The fact that this was an otherwise beautiful weekend day in the middle of summer, and the bay would be crowded with boats, also weighed against me wanting to use the kayak. The conditions were downright frustrating given that the fish were present in good numbers and size. I needed a sheltered vantage point from where I could access fishable water with the wind on my back. A local inlet jetty quickly came to mind.

When I drove up to the jetty about an hour later I found several anglers fishing the ocean end of the rocks. The water there was deep, fast-moving, and a little rough. I assumed they were targeting bluefish, which could handle and be caught in those conditions just fine. My plan to jig cast for fluke meant I needed to be looking for shallower and slower moving water that I knew could be found on the bay end of the jetty, which was currently devoid of anglers.

As I approached the inlet's back corner, I studied the rip lines, which presented as narrow swaths of darker blue water sprinkled with white against a more uniform blueish-gray background. The fact that there was only a sprinkling of white caused by a periodic breaking of small waves told me that the water speed was indeed slower here. Still, there was significant current with water pouring into the inlet and moving from my right to left.

The water was clear enough that I could learn something about the relative depth by studying the color. Up-current of the main rip line the water was light in color, light brown to tan, as the sand bottom influenced its appearance. This transitioned gradually to dark green on the downcurrent side of the rip. Prior to leaving the house I studied the Google Earth aerial imagery and what I saw from the sky was consistent with what I saw in front of me while standing on the jetty rocks. There was a relatively shallow sandbar that dropped off, but I wouldn't know how deep until I felt it out with a jig. As is always the case on this kind of structure, the water will move faster over the shallower water. It was very easy to imagine fluke lined up on the deep end of the drop waiting for food falling off the bar edge like dogs waiting for scraps falling off a dinner table. The fluke could do this from the comfort of the deeper and slower moving water without having to expend much energy dealing with current. I needed to get my jig to the bottom quickly at the drop-off and keep it in the near-bottom fluke strike zone. I'd start with a 1-ounce bucktail tipped with a 4-inch Gulp Swimming Mullet. This swam about a foot behind another Gulp Mullet on a plain hook for the dropper.

The wind was stiff and on my right shoulder as I shot a cast slightly upcurrent and a little way past the shallow end of the drop-off. I engaged the bail immediately when the jig hit the water and lifted my rod tip to make contact. I watched the taut line carefully as the jig sank until I saw a slight twitch that gave away the exact instant it hit the bottom. With a sharp lift of the rod I got the rig moving and began a very slow retrieve with a simultaneous rapid jigging motion with my 7 1/2-foot spinning rod. The rig took longer than I anticipated to reach the bottom and swept downcurrent faster than I expected as I barely cranked the reel handle. When the jig was slightly downcurrent, I stopped the retrieve entirely to allow it to sink back to the bottom.

The fact that this took more than five seconds told me that my jig was not heavy enough for this depth at this stage of the tide. No problem. I was carrying a wide range of jig weights.

My next cast was made with a 1 1/2-ounce jig. This one reached the bottom much faster, and judging by the angle of the line and reduced speed of its downcurrent sweep, was swimming significantly deeper. I stopped the retrieve momentarily to feel for the bottom, and it touched in about three seconds. The extra half ounce made a world of difference, and I felt I was in the strike zone the whole time now. About a third of the way into the retrieve, the jig broke out of the main current and into the slower moving water that bordered the jetty. I could now work it all the way to the rocks. To accommodate the slower water and up-slope bottom approaching the rocks, I picked up the cranking speed slightly while maintaining the rapid jigging motion. The jig became "stuck" for a second, but I detected enough give to realize this was a fish as opposed to a snag. I set the hook fast and hard, and the head shake left no doubt this was a fluke. I pulled and cranked hard in an effort to get it up and away from the snag prone rocks. Its sizable brown shape against the dark backdrop of the submerged jetty rocks was a nice sight. I kept steady pressure as I descended to a predetermined landing spot at the base of the jetty where my net lay waiting. A gentle bulge of water put the 20-inch fish in easy reach and into the net.

The next thirty minutes or so produced a steady pick of 14- to 18-inch fluke, and an equal number of sea robins. Some of the fluke came from the edge of the drop-off, but most were along the slope near the jetty. After awhile I noticed that the downcurrent portion of the retrieve was producing almost all sea robins, so I began avoiding that area. As the current slowed, the 1 1/2-ounce jig began making a lot of contact with the bottom to the point that I needed to increase the retrieve speed in order to keep it from dragging. It was time to drop down to a 1-ounce jig. The first cast after going back to the lighter jig took longer to hit the bottom, as expected, but I could keep it down on the desired slow retrieve because the current had decreased significantly from when I started. I moved it just a few feet before I felt unexpected slack on the line and buried the hook, realizing that this was a fluke that had grabbed the rig and kept its forward motion. It

This dark-colored jetty rock is slippery. Non-slip footwear is a must.

seemed strange to swing hard at the feeling of nothing, but the result was another nice fish in the cooler.

As is often the case, the bite picked up as the water slowed. Now the fish could take advantage of the ability to feed without having to expend much energy dealing with the current. The slower water also meant more available bait near the jetty. This is because the juvenile fish of many species that inhabit the rocks also take advantage of the window of slower water to come out of their sheltered holes to feed easily. This plays out perfectly for fluke, which can camouflage and partially bury themselves in the sand while they wait to ambush prey that swims by. This is the time of greatest potential to hook a large fluke from a jetty.

With the water moving slowly now, I made a cast just slightly upcurrent. The rig went unmolested as it came at me in almost a straight line, until it approached some submerged boulder rocks. The sharp hit was instantaneous, and it was clear from the hookset that this fish was a different size class from what I'd been catching. I put as much pressure as I dared on the 20-pound-test braid in an effort to keep it away from the jetty rocks. As it lay on the surface I steered it carefully to the landing spot, and it lunged for a dive that took a little line off the reel. I got to the water's edge as fast as I could safely while trying to maintain a bend in the rod. As I grabbed the net the fish rolled on its back exposing the big white underside while thrashing on the surface in a way that I feared would shake the hook free. With a little luck and good positioning, I was able to slide the 26-incher into the net with little room to spare.

Inlets are among the most productive pieces of water available to anglers. The one that I fished here is typical in that it's the passageway for water filling a bay on the rising ocean tide, and draining it as the tide drops. You can think of inlets as gamefish highways, for many species, as they ride the currents back and forth and feed on the plethora of bait that also use the inlet to move between bodies of water. While this particular inlet connects a bay with the ocean, smaller inlets that connect lesser bodies of water offer comparable angling opportunities. One of the primary reasons is the availability of food. Baitfish use the inlets as passageways, and many bait species spawn in the protected smaller waters. As this was August in the Northeast, I knew this was

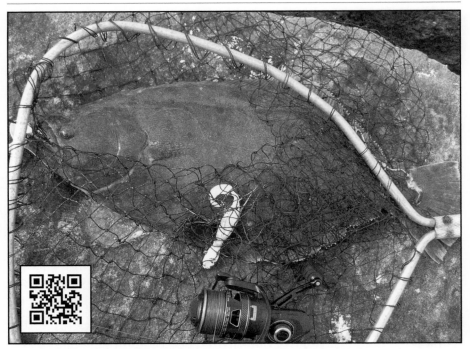

A quality jetty fluke. Choose the safest landing spots before fishing.

working to my advantage because juvenile bluefish, often called snappers, were born in the bay within the preceding month and had grown to perfect 4-inch forage fish that were high on the fluke's menu. While inlets offer anglers excellent fishing, I consider them among the most technically challenging fishing environments.

With four publicly accessible inlet jetties within a reasonable drive of my home, choosing which one to fish involved understanding how they were oriented to the day's wind. The wind was blowing from the southwest, so I immediately crossed off the two jetties that faced west, as I would much rather have the wind on my back for fluke fishing than be forced to cast into it. As with my beach efforts, my striper fishing tendencies that often drew me to windy and rough inlet water needed to be adjusted for fluke. My second consideration revolved around this being a little too nice a summer weekend day. One of the inlet jetties that met my requirements was so easily accessible that I could expect it to be mobbed with anglers of all kinds. The other required a six-mile off-road trip that was rewarded with plenty of room to fish.

This trip was on the deeper end of the range that I usually fish from shore for fluke. I think that would be true for most anglers. Judging by how long my jig took to sink and the slow retrieve that was required to keep it near the bottom, I'm guessing that I was fishing close to 15 feet of water in the deepest part of the retrieve. This called for the heavier jig and required that I fish a part of the tide window when the current was relatively slow. When I fluke fish inlet jetties I'm carrying bucktails weighing between 3/4 and 2 ounces. It is rare that I go heavier than an ounce and a half.

I used a slightly heavier spinning outfit here than I normally would for fluke casting. The possibility of needing to use heavier jigs was one reason, but I was more influenced by the desire to lift undersized fluke and sea robins from the water to the top of the jetty without having to keep climbing up and down the rocks. Most of these short fluke were in the 14- to 17-inch range, and some of the larger sea robins probably weighed more than these, so I needed to be able to swing a couple of pounds without worrying about breaking the rod. My choice was a 7 1/2-foot Penn spinning rod rated 12- to 20-pound-test line, matched with a Penn Clash 4000 spooled with 20-pound-test braided line. Whereas my fluke leaders are almost always tied from 20-pound-test Fluorocarbon, I use 25-pound-test leaders on jetties to help absorb the inevitable nicks and frays that occur when the rig rubs against the jetty rocks. No matter how hard you try to avoid this, the leader usually hits the rocks at some point, often when landing a fish. I almost always use 7-foot rods for fluke casting, but the slightly longer 7 1/2-footer that I use on the jetty helps keep hooked fish off the rocks.

Understanding and anticipating the current is one of the most important aspects of fishing an inlet. A tide calendar will tell you the times of high and low tides, but it will take some familiarity with the inlet you're fishing to know how that translates to when slack water occurs. High slack water is the period between incoming and outgoing current when the water stops moving before changing direction. The inlet that I fished in this story experiences high slack water approximately two hours after the time listed on the tide calendar for high tide. Low slack occurs almost three hours after low tide. It can be difficult to understand how the current can be rushing in while the tide is dropping, but this occurs because the bay behind the barrier island is rather large and is being fed by a narrow inlet. Its height lags behind that of the ocean. So even though the water level of the ocean may have started to fall, the bay's height still needs time to catch up.

Most tide charts have two pieces of information associated with a high or low tide: the time it occurs, and the height above or below mean low water. For example, if the number "2.9" accompanies the time of high tide, this means that the water height at high tide will be approximately 2.9 feet above the height of an average low tide. These numbers change with the moon phase, and can be used to help anticipate current speeds. Over time, I've learned that the current at the inlet in the story on a 3.0 is about average, above 3.5 is screaming, and below 2.7 is relatively slow. Being able to anticipate the current speed helps me choose where and when to fish, and what weight bucktails to bring. Extreme weather exerts some influence over the current speeds and the times of slack water, but under normal conditions, the numbers are dependable. The only way to get a handle on the tidal characteristics of the inlets you fish is to put your time in, keep track of posted tide times, and note when the slack periods occur.

When I fish an inlet jetty for fluke, my ideal timing is to fish roughly ninety minutes on either side of slack current, and through slack current itself. I mention ninety minutes because in just about any area of moving water the current starts slowing approximately ninety minutes before slack water. Because I'm always targeting the slower water when fluke fishing inlets, I consider this roughly three-hour window to be prime. This doesn't mean that the portion of the tide when the current is running at full speed is worthless. A possible solution at that time is to seek out features like bends in the jetty that might deflect the water and slow the current, or cause a fishable eddy.

During the three-hour tide windows that I suggest fishing, the current speed is in a state of flux. The fact that the current speed is changing constantly is one of the most interesting aspects of fishing an inlet. Even if I've been fishing for awhile without success, I know that the fish might turn on at any time when the current speed moves into a range that triggers them to feed. Because I suggest fishing through slack periods, I'm encouraging the angler to fish both incoming and outgoing current. Which is best? There's no clear answer, because it depends on the inlet's structure and other factors, such as the time of year, water temperature, and water quality. The impact of inlet structure on a current direction change is probably the most important of these.

One of the jetties that I fish runs straight south to north, from the ocean to the bay, for about the first half of the length of the jetty. It then takes a very slight bend to the northwest. On incoming current the water north of the bend, on the bay side, moves slower than the rest of the inlet. Looking at the inlet from the sky, it's easy to see why. The water runs straight north, down the first part of the inlet, but the bend in the jetty prevents the main flow from running along the rocks on the bay end. Satellite imagery also shows clearly that the area out of the main current has a shallow sand buildup. So this entire half of the jetty is ideal on incoming current because both the depth and current speed are manageable for fluke jigging from the rocks. However, everything changes when the current direction turns around and starts running out. Now there is unobstructed ebb current on the bay end of the jetty, but a slight deflection of that current on the ocean end. When I fish this jetty, I'm fishing north of the bend on incoming current, and south of the bend on outgoing. The water north of the bend appears to be less than 10 feet deep, and is fished properly with 3/4- or 1-ounce bucktails depending on current strength. When I move south of the bend I have to deal with slightly deeper water and jigs in the 1- to 1 1/2-once range.

Water temperature and quality can change drastically with a change in current direction, and this can have a significant impact on the fishing. This can often be observed if you fish the end of outgoing current and then for some time into the incoming. This is especially true during the warmer summer months when the bay water is significantly warmer than the ocean. At that time of year outgoing current is flushing warmer and usually more turbid water to the ocean. The turbidity comes from the higher levels of algae that are typically present in the bays. Go to the jetty at the end of outgoing and you might find brownish water that's difficult to see through. A couple of hours later, clear and cooler ocean water might be pouring into the inlet. While it seems logical that fishing the clear cooler ocean water would be more productive, this isn't always the case. I've had several trips when the fishing was good in that brownish end of ebb water but then slowed when the water cleared on the flood. I've also had trips that were great on the flood but then had the fishing shut down when the current turned. My point is to understand and anticipate changes in water quality, but don't have any preconceived notions as to which conditions will produce the best fishing.

Suspended weed can be a major fishing problem in some areas, making it next to impossible to have an offering in the water for any length of time without getting fouled. Sometimes this condition will clear up, or get worse, in response to a current change. Weeds usually come from the bay, and in such cases, outgoing water can be difficult to fish. However, I've experienced times when the opposite was true and weeds that were piled on the beach or floating in the ocean fouled the inlet on incoming. Again, anticipate that the current change might have a fishing impact, good or bad.

Whereas in the previous beach chapter I stressed the advantages of continuously moving to cover a large portion of the shoreline, jetty fishing is often more stationary. One reason is that the fluke often respond to the combination of structure and current by congregating in specific spots. If you're positioned well, you might have several of these potential hot spots in front of you without the need to move. When I fish an inlet jetty, whether for fluke or stripers, I see the water in front of me as a collection of potential hot spots. There were at least three in the inlet story. The first was where the incoming water was going over the drop-off. Another was the upward slope from the channel to the base of the jetty. As I'll write many times in this book, fluke love edges, and this transition from the main channel bottom to the shallower water where sand had built up along the jetty represented such an edge. Another potential productive zone was more difficult to work, but held a lot of promise. This was the rock-strewn bottom immediately adjacent to the jetty. Big fluke are often caught along this type of hard structure because it harbors all sorts of baits that the big flatties can handle. These include small bergals, sea bass, and crabs that often infest these rocks. The problem for the angler is that this structure presents unforgiving snags, and even if your jig makes it to the base of the jetty, it can be a challenge to reel it up fast enough so that it doesn't get caught on the rocks. If snags are a major problem but you know the fish are there, consider removing the dropper hook. This will reduce your odds of hanging up, especially when a fish swims your rig into the structure.

Cast placement and proper positioning on the jetty are key to productively working those pieces of water that are likely to hold fluke. In the story, the edge of the bar was visible from the jetty by observing the water color, but even if the water wasn't as clear, the rip line gave it away. I positioned myself slightly downcurrent of the drop-off, and cast a little over it to the shallow side. Standing downcurrrent allowed the jig to sink faster as it was pushed toward me. By the time it hit bottom it was still a little upcurrent of where I stood and I was in a good position to start the retrieve. Because the water nearest the jetty in this case moved slowly in relation to the outer water, I was able to work the jig all the way to the rocks. Short casts are sometimes needed to work the water close to the rocks if the current is substantial. It's important to vary the distance of your casts in order to target different pieces of water. Casting to the same spot repeatedly is rarely the best strategy.

I can't overstate the importance of being cautious when doing this kind of fishing. Jetty fishing can be dangerous. Even though fluke anglers typically fish calmer conditions than anglers targeting other species, such as stripers, they still may need to get to the water's edge to land a nice fish. Non-slip footwear is essential, and should match the most slippery portion of the rocks you'll be fishing on. For example, any decent pair of sneakers might be good enough on the dry clean top of a jetty, but they're a disaster waiting to happen down below where weed growth can create slippery surfaces. I wear felt soled wading shoes on the jetty, but spiked footwear might be more appropriate in areas where the weed growth is dense and your shoes need to bite into it. Waders should be avoided on jetties. Because this is relatively warm weather fishing, I'm often dressed in standard flats fishing clothes that protect from the sun and cover enough skin to minimize the annoyance of bugs. I highly recommend wearing a low profile inflatable PFD on the rocks. For less than $100 you can be assured that if you end up in the water, you'll at least be floating. These are so comfortable that you'll forget you're wearing one. Know where you'll land a nice fish before you hook up. Your first glimpse of a 5-plus-pounder at the edge of the rocks is not the time to be thinking about where to land it. I often choose where to fish on a jetty partially by considering where I'll be able to land a fish. A long-handled net can help keep you a little higher off the water and out of danger when closing the deal. Finally, have that net well-positioned while you're fishing. You don't want to be fighting a fish and carrying the net while you're scrambling down the rocks.

Inlet jetties offer great opportunities for shore-bound fluke anglers because they're often easily accessible and border on very productive water. Dealing with the differing currents, depth, and structure makes the inlets as challenging as they are productive. I'll leave this area with a few pieces of parting advice. Jetty rocks are frequently abrasive because they're covered with mussels and barnacles. This leads to nicks and frays of leaders – don't be lazy and overlook these. You'll feel very bad if you fish with a damaged leader and then break off a quality fish because of it. Try as best as you can to fish at least a little time on both sides of and through slack water. This often produces the largest fish. Be patient and optimistic when the fishing is slow. Keep in mind that the current speed is changing through a substantial portion of the tide cycle, and a good bite can develop at any time. Understand that there are portions of the tide cycle in which the water is simply moving too fast to accommodate the style of fluke fishing described here. In that case, think about easier fishing opportunities that might be present nearby. Let's head into the bay and check out one of these places.

Understanding tides and currents is key to jetty fishing success.

CHAPTER 6
BAY SHORELINES, FLATS, AND DOCKS

"Looks like a cuda," I thought to myself, as my eyes picked up the 3-foot skinny dark object against the light sand background. I stalked it from downcurrent, wading quietly through the knee-deep water. At about 25 feet away I decided to end my little game, and walked on past the submerged log as I proceeded up the shallow flat. I knew all along that there was no chance that the motionless shadow was actually a barracuda, as I was at least 1500 miles north of where I should expect to see any. Still, the shallow expanse I was wading across in my flats clothes made me feel more like I was in The Keys than in a Northeast bay. I figured it wouldn't hurt to pretend for a few moments.

The flat extended to my left for as far as I could see, and was cut by a channel that curved off from my right and into the distance directly in front of me. This flat was undoubtedly built up from sand washed in from the ocean through the nearby inlet, which was less than a mile away. While the flat might have looked rather featureless at a glance, closer inspection revealed varying structure of small channels and depressions that were deep enough to transport baitfish. The little cuts and dips were certainly sufficient to hold small stripers, but all I could imagine were the fluke that were likely camouflaged in the sand and waiting for bait to wash by. It's a scenario and environment that exists in many areas along the Flounder Coast.

Both the inlet and the open beach were a little too rough this particular afternoon. It was sunny and hot, with temperatures breaking

90 degrees on land, but the moderate onshore breeze caressing the cooler ocean water made the bay wading quite comfortable. With the water temperatures running unseasonably warm, I was betting that the fish were feeding best in the cooler incoming current. Over the past couple of weeks I had noticed Arctic terns working in the bay near the top of the tide. The activity of these small seabirds was almost a sure sign that sandeels were being pushed into the bay on this stage of the tide, as they were the predominant baitfish at the time and rather plentiful in the nearshore ocean. I planned to fish the last ninety minutes of incoming current and then a little way into outgoing.

As tempting as it was to wade the flat and fish its widespread and varied structure, I decided to focus on the main channel. As I do with all of my shallow water fishing, I surveyed the area with Google Earth in advance to get a mental picture of some of the features that might be visible from above but not at water level. The position of the channel edge was obvious from both perspectives, but the subtleties in the way it bent were more obvious from above. The satellite view also got me interested in an area where there was a gentle drop-off running perpendicular to the channel edge. I would start there, because this location would give me two interesting features to work on – the channel edge, and the bar drop.

I had been through this area a couple of times over the years by kayak, and didn't recall the water ever exceeding ten feet. I was far enough back from the inlet that the current speed was always suitable for fluke casting. This would be much easier fishing than having to fish around the current in the inlet. A 3/4-ounce bucktail tipped with a 4-inch Gulp Swimming Mullet would be a good starting point. The 7-foot Penn spinning rod rated for 10- to 17-pound-test line was a good match to the rig, conditions, and fishing. A Penn Conflict 4000 spooled with 15-pound-test braid balanced the outfit.

As anticipated, the incoming current that had been pumping in clean ocean water for the last few hours resulted in clear enough bay water that I could easily read the structure that I was interested in. Google Earth guided me to this general area, but the color of the water and the surface rip lines refined my positioning. I lined myself up on the channel's edge so that I had a light-colored patch of water upcurrent that transitioned to darker water downcurrent. This was the bar edge that ran perpendicular to the channel. The bar wasn't all that shallow, and probably had at least four feet of water flowing over it. The dark water gave me the impression that the bottom of the channel might be at least partially muddy. Bay mud often holds shrimp and small crabs, so it was an easy call to go with a Gulp Shrimp on the dropper hook.

I fired my first cast onto the bar and waited a couple of seconds to start my usual rapid jigging motion. The rig made it down the bar slope unscathed, and I paused the retrieve for a second to allow the jig to make brief contact with the bottom to confirm I was in the strike zone. I felt an immediate grab as soon as I resumed the retrieve, but the fish let go. I maintained the rapid bouncing and slow cranking as if nothing had happened. A few cranks later the fish bumped again. My rig was now getting close enough to where I was standing that I worried the high angle of the rod might cause the jig to ride too high, so I dropped the rod parallel to the water with no interruption of the retrieve. The fish had no intention of watching its prey escape into the shallows and hit hard on the bar edge. I buried the hook and pulled the fish over the sand bottom of the shallow side of the channel. The 19-incher was a respectable start.

I was surprised that the next two casts went untouched, so I moved slightly upcurrent so that my rig would go over some new bottom. As the rig slid to my downcurrent side the rod arched over with immediate weight. At first it felt like I had hooked a spider crab, but a couple of sharp head shakes erased any doubt. The fish put up a lot of resistance as I dragged it over the channel edge, but it wasn't until it was right in front of me that the 6-pounder turned and made a run. Had my drag not been set properly, something definitely would have broken.

The bite was solid for the next thirty minutes as I focused on a fifty foot stretch that allowed me to fish the bar slope. When that bite slowed, I fished my way downcurrent, attempting to cover all of the bottom on my way to a slight bend in the channel. The fish were plentiful and seemed evenly distributed as I covered an additional two hundred feet of channel edge. As with just about all fluke fishing environments, it pays to cover ground because the fish themselves aren't likely to be moving much. I could imagine a dozen or so fluke hanging along the bar edge, but after running my rig through there for a half hour and catching and losing that many, I had trouble thinking there were many

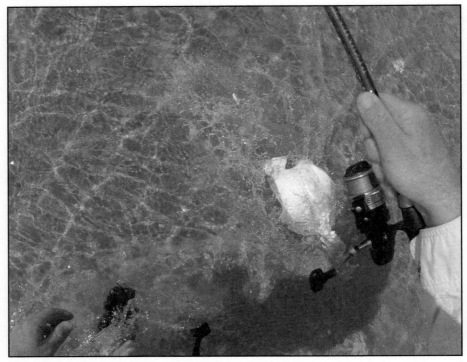

Big fluke can get feisty when dragged into the shallows.

fish left there that hadn't seen or dealt with my rig. Exploring new bottom seemed like a much more productive strategy, especially when there was so much good bottom in the area.

As long as I kept moving, the fishing remained strong into the first breaths of the ebb current. Then I could see the change with my eyes as easily as I could feel it with my now lifeless fishing rod. As the outgoing flow increased, the water visibility decreased and suspended weeds became a problem. The weeds weren't so bad that I couldn't fish through them, but the fish had turned off. I couldn't know whether this was due to an increase in water temperature or a decrease in clarity, but I knew my short though productive trip was finished.

If my life depended on catching a large number of fluke while standing on the shore or wading, I would choose this exact setting of sandbars and channels in close proximity to an inlet. The bars, channels, and differing bottom compositions all being flushed alternately by bay and ocean water offer the fluke plenty to eat in the presence of varied structure, while offering the wading angler easy fishing conditions and

Bay shorelines in many areas, especially near inlets, offer easy and productive fishing.

a fresh supply of fish coming through the inlet. It doesn't get much better than this. An unfortunate fact of this setting is that a lot of the easy wading structure is inside the bay a little ways and can't be reached from the shore. We'll fish in the kayak in the next chapter, but it's time to press it into service for transportation. A kayak will provide access to a tremendous number of wading options, even some that are so shallow that a kayak is the only way to get at them easily.

It's no secret that the areas immediately inside inlets are fluke hot spots in many areas of the Flounder Coast. One only needs to observe the dozens of boats that often congregate in these areas on any weekend during the fluke season. The number of boats fishing the inside is usually proportional to the size of the waves on the outside of the inlet. When the ocean is rough, the bay becomes the only option. It's also no secret that the bay channels hold a lot of the fish, so many boats will be fishing the channels. Because the channels are also highways for pleasure boats, they see a lot of traffic not even related to fishing. Some of these areas get mighty crowded and I've learned from experience that I don't want any part of them while sitting on top of my kayak. Standing in knee deep water with uninterrupted access to the structure the boats are jockeying for is another story.

Only a short paddle from the truck separated me from the sand and water playground where I would spend the afternoon. Whereas trips in which I'd be fishing from the kayak required some rigging and setting up of the fishfinder, I needed only to add a rod, surfbag, and wading net before pushing off. Although I had only a few hundred yards to cover, almost all of it was deep enough for the boats to be speeding through, so I kept a sharp eye out for any that might intercept my path as I paddled harder than usual to get across the channel quickly. It was a good feeling to see the water under the yak go from a dark green to light tan as I passed from the channel into the safety of less than three feet of water on the sandbar. In another minute I exited my little ferry and dragged it high and dry onto a small sand island. I felt almost silly as I carefully set an anchor on dry sand, but I knew how fast the island would be swallowed by the ocean water pouring through the inlet, a half-mile away.

If you had never seen this bay before, the thirty or so boats running up to the bar edge and then drifting back into the channel would be a dead giveaway that this was a hot spot. Even without the boats, this general area was a no-brainer as water poured over extensive flats and then filled a channel that began in a direct line from the inlet before gradually curving into the back bay. Private, charter, and party boats were all here, and so were the fluke. I felt almost as though I was cheating as I realized that by wading the bar, I had the very best water within casting distance, yet I wouldn't have to keep running back to the channel edge every time the current pushed me too far back as the boats needed to do. And while their drift was not quite optimum because the wind was blowing perpendicular to the current, every one of my casts could be placed right in the money spot where the bar transitioned to the deeper channel. With over a quarter-mile of easy wading available along the curved channel edge, I could spend a couple of hours just trying to cover it once through. It was hard to ask for a better situation.

Some trips take finesse in offerings, positioning, and presentation in order to put together a good catch. Most of the several hours spent on the bar this day saw *stupid fishing*, as most casts produced a fluke. With the current almost directly on my back, I needed only to cast a 3/4-ounce bucktail and dropper rig on a slight angle along the edge of the bar and crank very slowly with the rapid jigging action. Most of the hits came as the current pushed the jig into deeper water where the fluke were waiting. If I somehow managed to not catch one that way, then one would almost certainly grab on late in the retrieve as I tried to work the rig back up the bar edge. I typically avoid working lures into current, but in this setting I eventually had to reel into the current to retrieve the rig. Given the number of fish cruising the bar slope it made sense to just cut the retrieve speed down to almost nothing so that the rig bounced nearly stationary in the current. It was hard not to catch them. If there was any downside, it was that out of the easily seventy five fish landed, the largest were just a few in the 19- to 20-inch range. The majority of the fish were 14 to 17 inches. I did cover some ground even when I was catching well in hopes of finding some larger fish, but found the size to be pretty uniform no matter where I was fishing. I kept a close eye on the boats and didn't see them doing any better on size. I was confident that I bested them on numbers.

While I may beat the usefulness of Google Earth to death in these shallow water chapters, if you had never fished the bay I just wrote about you could have easily surveyed the prime structure from the sky. Even if you didn't know how to read this structure, you could simply use Google Earth's historical imagery tool to see many aerials taken over the years. What good is that? Consider that you could then look at these waters during the good fluking months and note where the fishing boats were concentrated. Even to someone with no experience on these waters, it would be pretty obvious that there was good fishing within easy reach of wading water.

I stayed near the main channel edges in these accounts of bay fishing.

On the higher end of a rising tide, fluke often move onto the flats to feed, and this can present some excellent opportunities to wade areas that are too shallow for most boats to reach easily. It can be very pleasurable to get far away from the boat traffic and wade these areas. As with fluke fishing in general, the key is to find the edges. One of my favorite spots has me casting to about two feet of water with a half-ounce bucktail rig and letting it sweep downcurrent to water that never exceeds four feet. The fish are in this spot in good numbers, and occasionally surprising size, near the higher parts of the tide. The rising tide is typically best for these shallow fluke, as they usually retreat to the channels when the water level drops. Although I've never tried it, some anglers do well fly fishing for these skinny water fluke.

Caution is required when wading bays. While it's usually obvious that the bottom is getting a little mushy, some of the soft spots are hidden on otherwise firm flats and don't look any different than the surrounding hard sand bottom. Proceed carefully and test the bottom as you go along, especially when you start seeing bottom color differences that might indicate a change in composition. I wouldn't be caught doing this fishing without an inflatable PFD.

Bays and harbors are often dotted with docks and piers. I view these structures as challenging places to target fluke because they're stationary, but some offer good opportunities. The vast majority of docks are private and constructed to provide boating access to homeowners and municipalities. Because fluke are widespread in many areas, and docks are often situated near boat channels, it sometimes happens by chance that these structures offer access to good numbers of fluke. Fishing piers are a little more likely to be productive because they're built for the purpose of fishing, and it's unlikely anyone would go through the expense of building one where there weren't any fish. I'll refer to both of these structures as "docks" for the next couple of paragraphs. Dock pilings will deflect current, and in areas with sufficient depth, may attract baitfish. If there's a fish cleaning station on the dock where people discard scraps of fish, this can be another bait draw. If there's a boat channel within casting distance, then you'll have a channel slope that might hold fish. Combine current breaking structure, interesting bottom contours, and the availability of bait with access to deeper water, and it's easy to see why some of these structures have good fluke

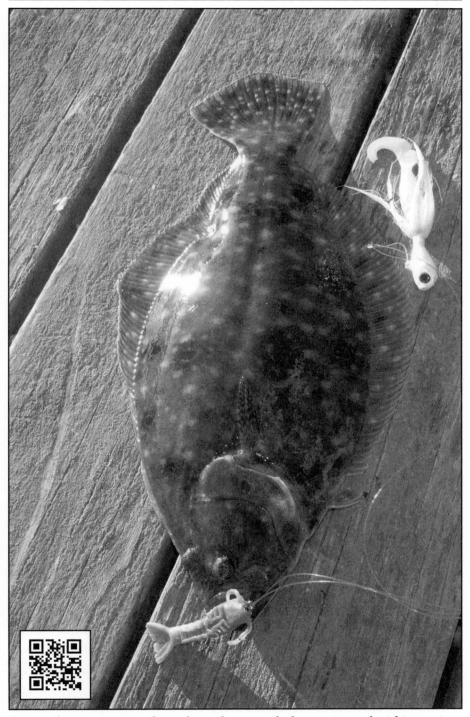

Due to their proximity to boat channels, many docks are situated within casting distance of good fluke fishing.

fishing potential.

If you have access to a dock or pier where fluke are caught, you can apply the techniques of this and previous chapters with some minor adjustments. Keep in mind that you'll likely be standing higher off the water and have deeper water beneath you than if you were shore wading. Whereas you always need to consider the water depth and movement of where your cast lands, you must now make adjustments for that higher and deeper vantage point. Because the angle of your line becomes steeper as your rig approaches the dock, the rig naturally wants to come off the bottom and out of the strike zone. This is where you need to make a conscious effort to keep your rig deep by slowing the retrieve or possibly stopping to allow your jig to touch the bottom. The video support for this chapter includes catching fluke from a dock where many of the hits come near the end of the retrieve. Because the water was around 7 feet deep where I was standing, I often stopped the retrieve when I was within about thirty feet of the dock to ensure the rig was near the bottom. Many of the hits came soon after I re-established the retrieve.

We've now fished from the open beach, to the inlet jetties, the bay shoreline, and farther back to the bay flats and bars. We've also considered the opportunities and challenges provided by docks and piers. There's a phenomenal amount of convenient shore-bound fluke fishing options, and a great deal more if you expand the territory by using a kayak as an access tool. If given the option of fishing a bay, jetty, or open beach on any given day, what would be the best choice? Let's assume that sea conditions are calm enough that they don't impact the fishing in any of these environments. If my goal was to catch the largest fluke, I'd target an inlet jetty around the slack water period. Inlets often hold quality fluke, and jetty structure can be an extra draw for the larger fish. As mentioned in the previous chapter, current speeds can be a limitation to being able to fish through an entire tide. If you have enough fishing time, a reasonable strategy is to fish the jetty in the hour or so on either side of slack current, and then move to the bay or open beach when the water moves too fast. If my goal was to catch a lot of fluke with less concern of catching a big one, I would opt for the bay most of the time.

Out of the three environments, I find the open beach to be the most challenging, but as the cover of this book shows, it can be very rewarding as well. In many areas it also offers the best shot at quiet solitude, since boats are not usually able or motivated to fish very close to the beach. You may need to do some walking to get away from swimmers in some areas. As with any kind of fishing, local knowledge goes a long way toward making the right call on which environment to fish for a given set of conditions and tides. Being proficient at catching shore fluke from a wide range of environments is an important step toward being able to stay productive through the season. If you long to push beyond the shore, the potential for good fluke fishing increases significantly. This can be achieved with modest cost and effort by adding a quality fishing kayak to your arsenal. Let's push off on top of a big piece of plastic.

CHAPTER 7
SHALLOW KAYAK APPROACHES

The day dawned calm and gray as damp air drifted inland off the ocean and left the bay covered by a light fog. The forecast was for it to burn off as the morning progressed. For now, there was just enough to eliminate the need for sunglasses, but not enough to delay my current task of unstrapping the kayak from the roof of my Jeep. Rigging the yak was a little more involved and required more time than when I used it only for transportation to get to my wading spots. The fishfinder and battery were connected, casting and jigging rods leashed in their rod holders, a landing net tucked against the hull by a bungee cord, a small cooler holding tackle placed in the tank well and secured with a safety line, and miscellaneous other items stored inside the hull. Within fifteen minutes of having pulled up to the shore of the bay, my GPS was touching base with the appropriate satellites and I was pushing off with a gentle incoming current.

I knew the general area well and had spent decades striper fishing the beaches on the opposite side of this barrier island, but this was the first time that I was fishing this bay for fluke. While fishing the nearby inlet jetty for stripers, I had often observed the for-hire and private boat fleet fishing for fluke a mile or so into the bay along the channel that carried water to and from the ocean. There was certainly no question that this place held a lot of fluke, and the kayak access couldn't be easier.

My lack of first-hand experience here was of no concern. I had a rough idea of where the good fishing took place, and was confident that given an hour or so I should be able to figure things out. For now, my focus was on a single mark on the plotter side of my GPS/fishfinder combo. I entered the waypoint into the unit manually the evening before after studying the area with Google Earth. Marine charts showed that water depths in this part of the bay ranged from 3- to 20-feet, from the top of a sandbar to the bottom of a channel.

While bottom structure that's close to an inlet can change frequently in response to storms, the stability of the structure increases as you move farther into the bay. Using the Google Earth distance measuring tool I learned that the area I was interested in was a mile from the back of the inlet, and three quarters of a mile from my launch site. The most recent satellite images were taken in winter, when the water was cold and clear. This gave me an excellent structure overview from the sky, with the light tan colored bar areas transitioning to a dark green in deeper water. There were patches of black that could have been mussel beds or darker mud bottoms. Given the distance from the inlet I could be sure that the structure hadn't changed much since the images were taken. The single set of GPS coordinates that I was paddling toward was arrived at by mousing over the middle of an interesting patch of structure while I studied the satellite imagery on my computer.

I chose the area because it was separated from the main channel by a sandbar, and there appeared to be a nice drop-off on the side of the sandbar that I was planning to fish. While studying the imagery I reasoned that bait moving with the incoming current would be pushed over the bar, and fluke would be waiting for them as the bar dropped off to deeper water. I would paddle the yak onto the bar, and let the current push me over and along the drop. Most of the boats would likely fish the main channel, and the larger of those would probably not be comfortable drifting over the shallow bar. While many kayak anglers don't mind, I try to avoid fishing on the kayak among larger boats, especially in a main channel that carries a lot of boat traffic.

With the help of the current on my stern, I was moving more than 5 mph while paddling with moderate effort. A light scattering of Arctic terns stretched well back into the bay and were hitting the water. When one crashed the surface nearby, I was very encouraged to see it come up with a sandeel in its beak. When the GPS indicated that I was about 300 yards from the mark, I turned broadside to the current and prepared to fish. The baitcasting rod was removed from the flush-mount rod holder and replaced by the landing net. After adding a Gulp Swimming Mullet to the bucktail and another to the dropper hook, I was ready to go. Because I lacked local knowledge, I started the drift well upcurrent of my target. This allowed me to get a better feel for the drift speed and direction, as well as some understanding of where the fish were situated. I would rather start the drift too early than overshoot the fish.

I dropped the rig to the bottom, only five feet below, and began rapid jigging with the 6-foot baitcasting outfit. In the minute or so it took to get my line in the water, the drift had stabilized and I was happy to see a 1.3 mph drift speed. I was initially a little worried that the current might be strong this close to the inlet, but the drift speed was well within the 0.5- to 1.5-mph range that I prefer. I expected it would slow a little as I drifted farther back into the bay. Given the shallow water and reasonable drift speed, a 3/4-ounce bucktail was a good match as the line angled out just slightly from the kayak. I misjudged the drift direction a little so I reeled up and paddled about fifty feet closer to the bar and channel, hoping that the adjustment would cause me to drift close to my sole GPS mark.

After five minutes of drifting without a hit, it was clear that I had not overshot the fish. I was slightly relieved when my jigging was finally interrupted by a sudden addition of extra weight. I set immediately with a hard lift, and the rod doubled over as the fish easily peeled 15-pound-test braid from the small baitcasting reel. Fluke always fight better when you're trying to pull them vertically, as opposed to horizontally as when casting. They're even more fun when you startle them in shallow water. After a couple of quick dives I slid the 21-incher into the landing net, and onto my fish stringer.

The next hit came in less than a minute, but the fish was a couple of inches short of the 18-inch legal size limit. There was a lot of weight on the next hit, which came seconds after my rig hit the water. I was thinking *5-pounder* when I saw a lot of commotion at the end of the line. I was just slightly disappointed to see it was a double header, as opposed to one larger fish. With both of them spitting up sandeels alongside the yak, I knew I was where I wanted to be, so I saved the position with the GPS. When it showed up on the plotter, I noticed it was less than a hundred feet from the one I had entered from the satellite imagery the prior evening. Two more fluke came up on the first drift, which I finally terminated when I drifted into some deeper water that wasn't producing any hits. Now I could start refining my drifts to stay on the fish.

I paddled hard upcurrent now, anxious to get back on the fish. The GPS showed 3.5 mph paddling upcurrent, which was fine by me. This meant that I would spend only about a quarter of my time paddling between drifts. I stopped about a hundred yards up-drift of my fish-proven GPS mark. It was a little beyond where I thought I hooked the first one, but even if I had gone too far I knew I would drift back onto the fish pretty quickly. It took about a minute this time, and again I was busy all the way back to where the water dropped down to 8 feet. I noticed that the current speed there had decreased to 0.7 mph, while most of the rest of the drift was in the 1.0- to 1.2-mph range. The bottom was also darker and softer feeling there, indicating more mud as opposed to the sand that I was catching over.

After several very productive drifts, the breeze came up and blew the fog away. The wind was almost perfectly inline with my drift direction, but the downside of that was it had pushed my drift speed past 1.5 mph, which is getting faster than I'd like. Among the items that I had stored in the hull was a small (30-inch) drift control sock. It's nothing more complicated than a canvas funnel, but is one of the most valuable fluke fishing aids that you can carry on a kayak or small boat. It was ready to go with a 15-foot length of rope attached. Before starting my next drift, I tied it to the carrying handle on the up-drift side of the kayak, threw it in the water, and watched it open like a parachute. I was pleased but not surprised to see the drift speed stabilize at about 1.2 mph. Drift socks are very effective on a kayak because it doesn't take much to hold a kayak back. Deploying this one reduced my drift speed by about 0.5 mph, and although this might not sound like much, it can make a world of difference when fluke fishing. Besides keeping your drift speed in a more productive range, a drift sock has additional value to a kayak angler because it reduces paddling (or pedaling) time. The slower the drift, the more time you actually spend fishing as opposed to paddling between drifts.

I spent hours on the fish, and surprisingly never found it necessary to make another GPS mark. There were a few dozen boats in the main channel, but I had no one near me until the top of the tide when a couple of the smaller outboards drifted over the bar and realized how good it was where I was fishing. There was plenty of room for everyone to fish comfortably and we all did well until the tide turned and killed the drift. A proper drift is a key ingredient to productive fluke fishing, and I had it on this trip. This was no accident. The trip was planned to have the breeze and current going in the same direction. Had the wind been blowing from the opposite direction, I would have fished the other side of the inlet to align the current with the breeze. I was ready with the drift sock when the breeze picked up. I was also ready when I glanced down at my GPS and saw that I was nearly stationary after the current change, as the wind was now blowing in opposition to the current direction. *Wind over tide* is how it's often called, although *wind against current* is more accurate.

Understanding that my kayak would not be covering ground anytime soon, I paddled to the spot I felt held the most fluke, and traded my baitcasting rod for a spinning outfit. It was rigged identically to the baitcaster with a 3/4-ounce bucktail rig, which traveled easily through the air on the first cast with the help of the breeze on my back. As I would when shore fishing, I watched the taut line carefully as the jig sank and initiated a rapid jigging motion on top of a slow retrieve as soon as a twitch in the line indicated the jig had touched bottom. As good as the drift jigging had been, this might have been even better as now I was catching on nearly every cast without losing any significant time paddling. Short moves were all that were required to stay on the fish, which hit aggressively through the first hour of the outgoing current. When the wind and current rose in unison to the point that the water got choppy, I decided to call it a very successful trip.

The kayak cut the little waves cleanly as I paddled back to the launch site with the current pushing from behind and the wind trying to hold me up. The fish that I kept were all still alive on my stringer, which was now covered by a wet towel in the tank well. The cooler full of ice that was in the back of my Jeep would be my first stop when I reached shore. I knew that I had caught a lot of fluke, but didn't realize

A nice catch from a shallow bay.

just how many until I reviewed the trip video and counted 91 fish.

Fishing productive structure was the key to success on this trip. Given the proximity to the inlet there was plenty of sand and current to combine to make some interesting features. With sandeels being pushed over the structure, the downcurrent sides of the bars were a good place to focus. It's worth noting that much of the hot fishing took place in only five feet of water. Once I drifted over a softer bottom where the water was only a little deeper and slower, the fish weren't there. Imagine this same area without the sandeels. Would the fish congregate in the same places? I got to find out a week later.

I thought I had the fish nailed down given my previous success fishing the sandbar area, but after several nearly fishless drifts over my formerly hot GPS marks, I began wondering if I had just been lucky. The drift was good, everything seemed right, but all I had to show for an hour's fishing were a few small fish. The one difference between this and the previous trip was that there was no sign of sandeels this time. I didn't see any in the water, and the few terns that were around were not diving. While thinking about what to do, I allowed the kayak to go beyond the normal end of the drift, and into the darker deeper water. I realized

I was out of the previous week's strike zone but decided to let the drift proceed. I needed to change something, and this deeper and slower water over what I believed to be a mud bottom was worth a shot.

The dark color beneath the yak made the water look deep, but the fishfinder showed nothing deeper than nine feet. The drift speed was just slightly slower than over the sand. Whereas the bottom bumps with the jig were sharp over the sand bottom, they were softened here, confirming that I was now over mud. When I first felt weight at the end of the line, I momentarily thought it was weed before a slight movement caused me to set the hook. The fish made a nice little run and a few dives before ending up in the net. Nothing big, but it wouldn't need measuring before being put on the stringer. I noticed immediately that the brown side of this fish was darker than the others I'd been catching. This one was a dark brown, as opposed to the tan-colored sand fish. As I was placing it on the stringer, its white bottom showed

A big fluke that hit a Gulp Shrimp over a mud bottom.

black smudges. This was clearly a mud fish. As I straightened the deck up I found a small partially digested crab that the fish spit up. I was anxious to paddle back up for another drift.

This time I stopped paddling when I hit the light-colored water, as this drift would be entirely over the mud bottom. It didn't take long to connect again, and this one spit out a mess of crab pieces as it thrashed in the net. Now things made sense. There were still fluke in the general area, but given the lack of baitfish being pushed over the bars and sand bottom, the fish had to switch to something else to eat. As they did on the open beach with the mole crabs, these fish had switched over to the numerous crab and shrimp species that inhabit the mud of a bay or harbor bottom. I'm normally content fishing white bucktails, but as soon as I realized they were on crabs, I switched to a 3/4-ounce orange and brown jig. Its manufacturer, S&S, calls it a sea robin pattern. With that jig and dropper hook tipped with Gulp Shrimp, I

 established a solid bite over the mud. It wasn't as hot and heavy as the fishing I had the previous week with the sandeels in the area, but it did produce a couple of larger fish over five pounds.

Later in the book we'll head out in my 16-foot tin boat to fish for fluke over the varied structure of Long Island Sound. With such a capable and easily trailerable boat sitting in my driveway, why would I constrain myself in terms of space and on-water mobility by fishing out of a kayak? It's a combination of practicality, convenience, and aesthetics. Yes, I can get my boat to the waters I fished in this chapter. It would require trailering about thirty miles and paying to launch at a private marina. Then I'd need to ride a few miles across the bay. On subsequent days when I've wanted to take my kids fishing, and this area looked like the best option, I did the boat thing. If I'm fishing solo I won't even consider the hassles and expense of the boat. Even though I can't travel over water much faster than 5 mph on a kayak, I can launch very close to the fishing. This is one of the beauties of kayak fishing. If you can park near the water, there's a good chance that you can find a spot to slip a kayak in. There are many more places where this is possible than there are boat launching ramps. The kayak convenience and widespread launching options allow for quick trips that can even be carved out of a workday. My day job employer

A properly rigged kayak provides access to varied fluke environments.

probably doesn't notice when I show up late or leave early with a kayak on top of my Jeep. I don't think it would go over as well if I parked my boat outside my office. Practicality and convenience aside, I see a much stronger motivation to fishing out of a kayak. Much of this is personal preference.

Kayak fishing is a very aesthetically pleasing way to fish. No noise, gas fumes, and in most cases, no chance of mechanical breakdown. As a lifelong surfcaster I can say that many of the intangible qualities that draw people to surfcasting are present in kayak fishing. It's not just you and your physical capabilities against the environment, it's you *with* the environment. Observing undisturbed marine life as you glide quietly across the water is a free added bonus to the actual fishing. The kayak angler's perspective of being at near eye-level with the water's surface as a fish is landed is unique and adds an extra level of excitement. Each fish landed in the kayak means more to me than if I had caught it in my boat. This is not meant to be a book about kayak fishing, however, a suitable fishing kayak can be a valuable tool in a fluke angler's arsenal. As extensive and productive as the shore-bound fluke fishing opportunities are, they still only scratch the surface of what's available if you move out of the wading depths. A kayak can be a convenient and cost-effective vehicle to do that, whether or not you already own a boat. A quick crash course in fishing kayaks is worth a little ink.

There are two main types of kayaks – Sit-On-Top, and Sit-In. By far, the majority of fishing kayaks are Sit-On-Tops. These are very safe in that any water entering the shallow cockpit drains immediately out scupper holes. Should you flip a Sit-On-Top kayak, it's easy to roll back over and climb back on without the worry of flooding or having to bail. There are many models made with fishing in mind, and these are very stable and easily outfitted with fishing aids such as rod holders and electronics. The Sit-On-Top kayaks then branch into paddle or pedal propulsion. Hobie makes pedaling models, and these are wildly popular among serious kayak anglers. Most of the rest are propelled by paddling. Among the more popular paddling fishing kayaks are those made by Ocean Kayak and Wilderness Systems. Fishing kayaks are typically in the 11- to 15-foot range, and weigh between 60 and 90 pounds.

Having surveyed kayak anglers while giving fishing seminars in the Northeast, I can write with confidence that the majority of serious kayak anglers in that region are fishing out of Hobie kayaks. These pedal-driven craft offer the advantage of hands-free fishing because you can hold a fishing rod at the same time you're propelling the kayak. The kayak I fished from in the story is a 15-foot Ocean Kayak Trident. This is a paddling kayak that is well laid out for fishing, including a recessed built-in compartment for a fishfinder. A feature that's very important to me provides access to the inside of the hull through a large cockpit hatch called the *Rod Pod*. This allows one to store and access rods and other gear easily while sitting in the cockpit.

Among the things to consider when buying a kayak are speed and stability. The wider the kayak, the more stable but slower it will be. A long narrow kayak will cut through a chop much easier than a shorter wider one. A prospective kayak angler has to weigh this stability vs. speed trade-off. Weight and price are other concerns. It can be a shock to someone looking for their first fishing kayak to learn that some cost more than a decent used boat, motor, and trailer package. On the other end of the price range are some very inexpensive kayaks commonly offered by major sporting goods chains. The best thing one can do when considering their first kayak is to demo or rent one from a reputable kayak shop where you can evaluate different models. Buying a used kayak that's not overly banged up can save a lot of money while not giving up any functionality.

To people who have never experienced a quality fishing kayak before, it's common that they envision it flipping. These kayaks are actually quite stable. In surveying kayak anglers, I've heard only rare accounts of anyone flipping, except when launching and landing in the ocean surf. Regardless of how unlikely it is that I'll ever flip my kayak, I'm always prepared for it. The first thing I did with each of my two kayaks when I first bought them was flip them intentionally so that I could understand the best way to right the crafts and climb back in. It should be obvious that a PFD should be worn at all times. I wear the same inflatable that I use on the jetty and for shallow water wading. Cold water is a big danger in some areas at certain times of the year. In these circumstances I'll wear a wetsuit. I keep my fishing tackle in a small 6-pack cooler so that, in the worst case, at least my tackle will be floating. *Leash it or lose it* is a phrase often heard in kayak angling, so I have a lanyard on anything of value.

A GPS/Fishfinder combo is a very important piece of equipment for any fishing kayak. Installing one is easier on some models than on others. On one end of the spectrum is the ease of adding a unit to my Ocean Kayak Trident. This has a molded compartment with a cover called a *Sonar Shield* to hold the unit, a battery storage bag in the bow hatch, and a transducer compatible scupper hole. By purchasing an appropriate Humminbird GPS/Fishfinder combo with a special

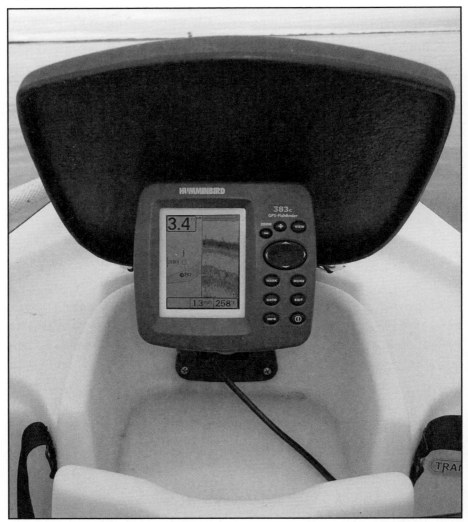

The Sonar Shield on the Ocean Kayak Trident provides shade and shelter for a fishfinder.

transducer that fits the scupper hole, installation involves little beyond screwing the unit's bracket into the Sonar Shield compartment. The battery is a simple 3.5-pound 12-volt Sealed Lead Acid (SLA) battery that fits nicely in the provided battery storage bag.

On the other end of spectrum is the situation that exists on many other kayaks in which there is no special accommodation for a fishfinder or transducer. In these cases you would need to do some research and then do a somewhat custom installation. My older Ocean Kayak Prowler fits that category, and required significantly more work to install the fishfinder than in the Trident model. It's usually not hard to find a place to mount the fishfinder unit, but the transducer installation can be a little more complicated. Fortunately, most fishfinder transducers can shoot through a kayak hull, so the transducer does not actually have to go in the water. You can instead mount it inside the hull, although you'll sacrifice the temperature reading. There are several ways to do this with plenty of instructions and videos online to help you along.

When the current direction changed in the first story, I stayed productive by switching from jigging to casting to deal with the wind against current situation. In a pedal kayak I might have been able to pedal slowly into the wind in order to keep my rig going in the right direction. In a boat you could slow troll, although I personally find that to be such an annoying way to fish that I simply won't do it. It's pretty hard to get an outboard to troll at such a slow speed, so you might need to alternate between neutral and forward. An electric trolling motor would be an excellent tool to deal with wind against current. The engine mount electric motors made by Minn Kota and others would be a perfect solution on an outboard.

When fluke fishing, I can't overstate the importance of keeping the rig moving in the same direction as the current, or at least have it moving across the current. Moving the rig against the current is rarely productive, and if it is, it's still probably less so than if you made adjustments to have the rig moving with the flow. Fluke lie on the bottom facing into the current as they watch for food being pushed their way. Having your rig coming up from behind the fluke is not only unnatural, it is difficult to do without adding substantial extra weight because the force of the water will be pushing the rig off the bottom and potentially high enough to be out of the strike zone.

Anglers with pedal kayaks have the option of fishing their way back to the beginning of each drift because they can pedal and jig at the same time. Although this might sound like a good way to keep a line in the water and stay productive, it is probably better to just pedal back up-drift at the fastest comfortable speed and avoid spending time making slow forward progress while dragging the rig against the current. You may catch a few going into the current, but you're almost sure to be better off by maximizing the amount of time you spend making proper drifts with the current.

Casting worked well for me in the first story when I was dealing with wind against current, but I've also found it to be more productive than vertical jigging when I've fished very shallow water that's less than four

feet deep. This has been especially true when fishing clear water. It's difficult to say for sure, but at some point it seems possible that the fluke are somewhat spooked by the presence of a kayak or boat just a few feet above them. They might not flee the situation, but it's been my observation that they're less likely to leave the cover of bottom and chase a jig. I've had slow fishing in these shallow clear water situations turn into excellent action when I switched from jigging right under the kayak to casting away from it and working the jig across the current.

Under normal drift conditions and over anything but very shallow and clear water, I'm going to be jigging with baitcasting tackle. I generally use the same 6- to 7-foot rods in my kayak as I do in my boat. One foot makes a significant difference in a fishing rod, and it's a personal preference as to whether you want to fish a shorter or longer rod. I prefer the 6-footer when shallow bay fishing in the kayak, because the fish are easier to reach when being landed. When we head into deeper ocean water in later chapters, I'll make a case for a 7-footer. Let's head out in the boat.

CHAPTER 8
SOUND STRUCTURE STRATEGIES

Lifeless. It's what I concluded after five minutes of drifting over a Long Island Sound sand shoal that was the local ground zero of the fluke fishery. Cold and very clear water, no birds overhead, a clean fishfinder screen, and not a bump on my bucktail rig. Not wanting to draw too fast a conclusion, I ran the boat in a hundred yards to fish over the shallowest part of the shoal. No change. The sandeels simply weren't there, and the fluke had no reason to be over this mostly barren bottom in their absence. Still, this was mid-May and there had to be fluke in the Sound. Without sandeels to draw them to their usual grounds, they would have to find an alternate bait source. Looking in at the boulder strewn beach a mile to my south, the next move seemed obvious. The waters close to the beach hid various concentrations of boulders and rocky rubble. These in turn held crabs and small fish, not unlike the ocean inlet jetties. In the absence of sandeels, these baits had the potential to pull fluke tight to the beach. I headed in, and didn't shut down until I was within 200 yards of the shore.

I chose an area away from the shoal so that I would have relatively deep water in close. Lobster trap buoys marked the heaviest of the structure, just inside of where I set up for my first drift. You can usually count on trap buoys to mark good fishing structure, but I was careful to stay clear of them so I wouldn't get snagged.

I stared intensely at my boat's fishfinder as I watched the nearly flat line of the bottom suddenly become ragged and then bulge slightly. I maintained the rapid jigging as I passed over the small hump, but lifted the rod a bit to try to compensate for the momentary rise in the bottom. I felt the jig stick for a second at the high point, but a quick flick of the wrist freed it. When I saw the falling edge of the bulge, I depressed the thumb bar on my reel to make sure I touched bottom again on the downcurrent side of the structure, and quickly resumed the rapid jigging. I felt a sharp tap, followed by weight, and set hard with the 7-foot baitcaster. The rod doubled over, but only briefly as the fish came off. I immediately resumed jigging, confident that the fish would come back. The next hookset was a reflex as the fish pounced on the jig a couple of seconds later. Line peeled off the small baitcaster and then paused, as a telltale head shake confirmed that this was a quality fluke. A tug of war ensued for the next minute as I would put a few yards of 15-pound braid back on the reel, but then lose some of it to a powerful dive. The 4-pounder was a nice start, and typical of the size of the fish that I often find near the rocks.

I motored back up to repeat the drift, and turned the boat broadside to the current. The slight breeze that I had on the first drift had picked up a bit, and was now blowing with the current at what felt like a little over 10 knots. I sent the one-ounce bucktail to the bottom with a lot of anticipation. After bouncing for about ten seconds, I hit the thumb bar to touch up with the bottom again. It took a few feet of line to get down. I had to repeat the process a few seconds later as the drift speed was now up to 1.5 mph, mostly wind-driven, and my line angle was starting to scope out. I quickly deployed a 44-inch drift sock that took care of the problem. Drift socks are made in different diameters for different size boats, and I intentionally bought one a couple of sizes larger than what is recommended for my 16-foot tin boat, but it does a great job in a stiff wind. A drift sock only diminishes the wind component of the drift. This is true because in the absence of wind, the drift sock and boat move at the same speed with the water, so it has no effect. What this means is that buying an over-sized drift sock will never slow you down more than the current speed, so it's better to be over-sized than under-sized when purchasing. Just remember to pull the drift sock out of the water at the end of each drift and tie it off securely in case you forget, which is easy to do.

The wind held steady, and the drift sock helped keep the boat drifting

Gulp shrimp are deadly, especially when fluke are feeding on shrimp and crabs.

near the 1.2 mph sweet spot. This allowed me to stay with the 1-ounce bucktail that I started with. I would have gone to a 1 1/2-ounce had line angle scoping become a problem as it had before I put the drift sock out. The bite wasn't fast paced, but as long as I drifted along the structure marked by the pot buoys, I hooked up every few minutes with a fish that was typically between 3 and 5 pounds.

I'll describe a specific area of Long Island Sound in this chapter that features a wide range of structure. I understand that most readers will never fish the exact waters I'm describing, but that's fine. This area was chosen because it will allow us to consider everything from rocky areas to sand ledges, troughs, and many features in between. While you might not fish this exact area, there's a good chance you'll fish some places with similar characteristics. Although I'll describe the bottom structure here in clear terms, this book's companion website links to numerous underwater videos of the varied structure in this area, complete with fluke reacting to the fishing techniques.

For those not familiar with the Sound, it has structure similar to many other bodies of water in the northeast and elsewhere. I'll focus specifically on a 30-mile stretch of water between Port Jefferson and Mattituck so that the reader can refer to a marine chart (#12354), but the structure I describe here pertains to much of Long Island's North Shore. The Sound waters here see varying concentrations of boulders and rock rubble within several hundred yards of the shore in depths to about 25 feet. Four large shoals push out at Port Jefferson, Rocky Point, Wading River, and Riverhead. The edges of these shoals vary in steepness, sometimes resembling small underwater cliffs where the water drops sharply from 12 to 90 feet. The drop is more gradual in other areas. The northern tips of these shoals are marked by navigational buoys, and it's these areas that see the bulk of the fluke fishing efforts for private, charter, and party boats. If you ran your boat for the mile and a half from the beach to one of these buoys, you'd probably have to watch for rocks in the early going, then you would go over varying bars and troughs for about a mile before reaching the outer edge of the shoal. The entire area is washed by a mild to moderate current that will push a boat up to a maximum of about 1.7 mph at peak current in the absence of wind.

No matter where you fish for fluke, you're almost sure to experience seasonal variations in the fishery. Fluke begin showing in these waters each year in early to mid-May. The best structure to focus on depends on the predominant bait at the time. It's mostly a sandeel driven fishery, as large concentrations of these baitfish usually pour into the area at some point in the late spring. The challenge for the fluke angler here is similar to one faced by anglers in many places – the arrival time and amount of bait is not consistent from season to season.

The setting of the opening of this chapter was the very beginning of the season. The waters were still cold, very clear, and the sandeels were nowhere to be found. You could scan the horizon of the shoal ledges with binoculars and not see a single Arctic tern. When the sandeels are in, it's typical to see hundreds of terns flying overhead and diving frequently to pick up these slender baitfish as they're pushed to the surface by various predators. While this type of bird activity almost guarantees the presence of sandeels, the lack of birds is not a total

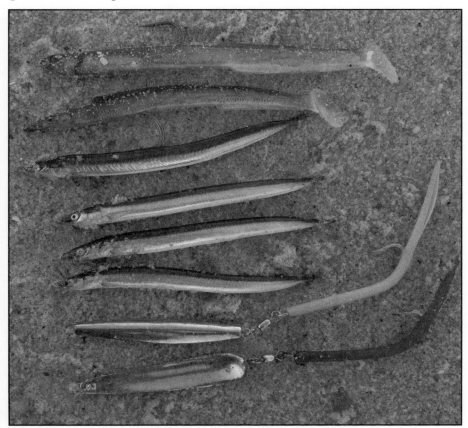

Sandeels fuel the fluke fishery in many areas of the Northeast.

certainty that the baitfish aren't there, but staying deeper. It's why I had to actually go out to the shoal and make a couple of drifts even though I could see from a distance that there weren't any birds working overhead.

When I ran inshore, I didn't need to go to the heaviest of the structure to find fish, as I would if I were targeting blackfish or sea bass. I needed only to get into an area where the bottom wasn't so clean and barren as it was on the shoal. If you view this chapter's support video, you'll see a lot of clutter from mussels, clam shells, and other debris on the bottom. All of this is sufficient to hold small crabs and juvenile fish that the fluke can feed on. Much of this life and clutter is too tight to the bottom to show up on most fishfinders, but if you pay close attention you'll be able to feel and find it with your jig. Simply let the jig drag bottom for several seconds and note whether it's smooth or bumpy. Sometimes the bottom debris is thick enough that you'll feel it without trying. Looking for the fluke's secondary food source is similar

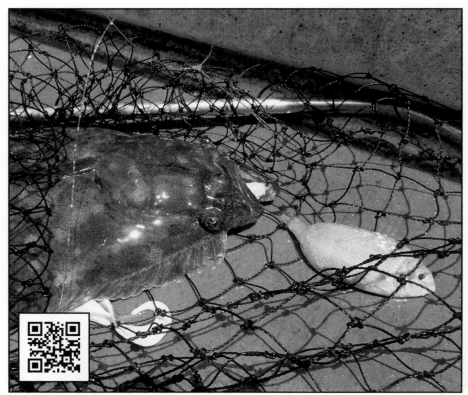

This quality fluke spit up a juvenile porgy

to the situation with the crabs on the lip of the ocean beach or the shrimp and crabs in the bay mud. Fluke are drawn to schools of baitfish, but in their absence, they'll seek out an alternative.

A week after catching well in tight to the beach, my college-aged daughter, Katie, joined me for a trip. I told her we wouldn't have far to run, as the fish were only about a mile down the shore and in very close. We pulled up outside the lobster buoys with the first breaths of the ebb current and a calm wind. We started with 3/4-ounce bucktails, but I expected to go up to an ounce when the current got rolling. Given the expectation of the fish being on crabs to some extent, we had Gulp shrimp on the teaser hooks. When the first drift produced nothing but a pair of sea robins, I suspected we had a problem. When only one small fluke came up on the next ten-minute drift, I knew we were out of there and would have to start searching. Because the current starts running close to the beach about forty minutes before it does on the outer end of the shoal, I took some consolation in realizing that our stop didn't cost us any tide.

Off we went on our anticipated three-mile ride that would have us running diagonally out from the beach to the end of the shoal. No GPS was necessary, as it was a very clear day and the big green can that marked the shoal would soon be visible on the horizon. We made it nearly two miles when I saw something unexpected – terns working the shoal about halfway out to the buoy. They showed up clearly against the vegetation-covered high bluffs that border most of Long Island's North Shore. I shut down and got out the binoculars. Sure enough, there were terns working the inside of the shoal, but none on the outside. Their presence could very well explain why the fluke weren't in the first spot, near the beach. If the birds were working sandeels, then the bait schools likely pulled the fish from the nearshore structure. It was part of the natural seasonal progression.

I changed course and headed for the birds, stopping where they were the heaviest. Our lines went down, but not far, as there was only 13 feet of water on this part of the shoal. We each barely got a bounce in when we doubled up. She was all smiles, but I knew almost from the hookset that this wasn't what we were looking for. Between the two of us we quickly had three sea robins on the surface, as Katie had a double-header. It seems most fisheries have an interference fish, and sea robins fill that job in the northeast fluke fishery. I took mine off and got Katie back in the water while I dealt with her double-header. She had two more waiting for me before I could get the second one back in the water. Even if the fluke were here, there was no way to get past the more aggressive sea robins. I immediately ran back upcurrent and set up a little farther out so that we wouldn't repeat the previous drift, but the result was the same sea robin inundation.

Heading for the thickest concentration of working birds isn't always the best move, and this seemed like one of those times. The birds don't tell you where the most bait is, they tell you where the bait is near the surface. Because fluke stay very close to the bottom, they are rarely responsible for pushing the bait all of the way to the top. Sea robins and bluefish are more likely to do this. We pulled our lines and I headed slowly north, toward deeper water, while watching the fishfinder. After about a minute, the bottom went from a steady 13 feet down a gradual slope to about 18 feet. Although the birds weren't as thick, there were clouds of bait near the bottom on the fishfinder.

It took less than a minute on the first drop for Katie to connect with a fish, and I was relieved to see the rod tip bounce in a way that indicated it was a fluke. It was an inch short of the 18-inch minimum limit, but encouraging nonetheless, especially since it spit sandeels all over as I swung it into the boat. Even though it was just one fish, I took a mark with the GPS to give myself a reference point, as I had never fished this particular spot before. It didn't take long for her to hook another one, and this one required measuring to see that it was only slightly short. As we drifted farther back, we went up the gentle slope and were soon back to 13 feet of water. When the next two fish were a sea robin and a very small fluke, I ran back up again. Because the first fish was caught early on the previous drift, I ran a little farther upcurrent in an attempt to find the upcurrent edge of where the fish were concentrated. I also ran a little farther out in order to stay on the deep side of the slope. We still didn't have a keeper in the boat, but I was working on refining the drift over this area that seemed to have potential.

We combined for another short and a sea robin at the beginning of the drift. It took me three swings to hook the next fish, but when I did, it had me fooled into thinking it was a striper on the initial run. It didn't take long to realize we'd be eating fluke tacos that night if I could put this one in the net. With Katie tied to her own fish, I was left to handle the netting myself with a fish that still had some fight left at the surface. I was careful not to rush netting it inappropriately, and certainly not from behind. It finally settled down, and with five feet of line left between the rod tip and the fish, I grabbed the net with my reeling hand and carefully pulled with my other arm to slide the big flattie in head-first. It pushed the scale past six pounds. I jokingly told Katie we only needed nine more for a limit. At that moment, I was just happy to have a meal.

Over the next two hours I zeroed in on the most productive piece of bottom, and kept the drifts short and focused. The fishing accelerated and we soon found ourselves processing fish almost as fast as we could

Head-first netting is the way to go.

handle them. We worked a little system that we started when my kids were around seven years old and were making their first boat trips. I would take care of all of the unhooking and care of the rigs, and they would just fish. This involved swapping rods each time they landed a fish, assuming mine was freed up and didn't have a fish of its own. This seemed the most efficient way to ensure that we always had a line in the water as much of the time as possible. When they were young it also minimized my worry that one of them could slip up and get a hook in the hand. The only downside of fishing this way is that my kids didn't get a lot of experience unhooking their own fish or dealing with the rigging. They did, however, hone their fishing skills and catch a heck of a lot of fish.

Light tackle fluke fishing is fun and easy for the kids.

Once we broke the ice with the first keeper, the others just kept coming, mixed with more than an equal number of shorts. What had started as a sea robin inundation and then just a pick of fish that were too small to keep progressed to the point that we found ourselves headed for home with a full limit of ten fish. The fish were about a mile from where I would normally find them near the deep edge of the shoal, clearly drawn to the area by the bait. Even though the birds easily gave away where the bait was, it took a little searching over the bottom structure to find the fish. As is frequently the case, a hundred yards made the difference between nonstop sea robins and a cooler full of fluke. While mine was the only boat on this off the beaten track area, more than a dozen boats fished along the more traditional fluke

A Gulp Swimming Mullet on the bucktail and a shrimp on the teaser hook give fluke a choice of baits to hit.

grounds near the shoal drop-off. Reports that I received the next day revealed that very little was caught there.

While patience is sometimes described as a virtue, I generally do not find this to be true in fluke fishing. As mentioned in the beach chapter, these fish do not cover ground as fast as some others. If you are not catching, they are not likely to come to you. It is your job to find them. If I'm not catching, I move. If I am catching and then go a minute or two without a hit, I'll run upcurrent to make a new drift in an attempt to locate and stay on the highest concentration of fish. Today's affordable electronics make this very easy. If I'm not totally locked in on a bite, I'll vary my drifts slightly in such a way that I feel I'm painting the bottom and always covering new ground. This helps me form a mental picture of how the fish are distributed. When I do find them, I pound the fluke concentrations with short drifts.

I'm not only aiming to catch legal-sized and larger fluke, I'm looking to avoid interference from the sea robins and smaller fluke. In other areas the interference might come from dogfish sharks and skates. In the same way that I'll move if I'm catching nothing, I won't repeat drifts over interference fish that are wasting my time. It might be tempting for anglers who have a fast-paced bite of small fluke to think that if they keep at it, they'll eventually catch some keepers. I find this to be flawed reasoning. Fluke seem to segregate by size to some extent.

A beautiful Black Sea Bass and some jumbo porgies mixed with the fluke jigging catch. These were accidental and tasty bycatch.

If I'm trying to catch fluke over 18 inches, and I'm catching 13- to 16-inch fish nonstop, those small ones are just wasting my time. In this situation I'll spend some effort making small drift adjustments while trying to find a bottom feature, such as a deeper trough or gentle slope. I'm looking for anything that can make a difference. If I spend an hour doing that and can't find size, I'll probably pick up and move away from the area.

The day after my daughter and I had the fish, a low pressure system moved in. No matter what fish I'm targeting, the forecast "Rain — Heavy at times" gets my interest. Unlike most of these weather systems, this one came in with very little wind, so it allowed me to get back on the fish. As good as Katie and I had it the previous day, it paled in comparison to the savage bite that took place in the rain. Although I started in the same area where we had them, I ended up more than a half-mile down the shore when I settled in on the main body. The *20 fluke in 18 minutes* video that I referenced in Chapter Three was recorded on this trip. On my way back to the launching ramp I made one last drift over the same GPS marks where Katie and I had the fish, and came up empty. These fish were clearly on the move, which is common in these waters in the beginning of the season.

Within a week this whole area died, as the bait and fish settled in on the outer part of the shoal near where it drops to deep water. This is interesting structure because you can be fishing in 15 feet of water and then a half minute later you're in 90 feet. The slope of the shoal varies as you approach the edge, and almost all of the fish are caught in less than 40 feet of water. Sometimes they're on the flat part of the shoal, but other times almost all of the quality fish are on the slope. By targeting the portion of the shoal edge where this slope is relatively wide, it's easier to keep a drift on the slope and in the productive area. Out of all of the places that I fish in the Sound, this is the piece of structure where precision drifting can make the most difference. Many times I've put together quality catches on the slope while boats a hundred feet away and making long drifts on the flat part of the shoal had only small fish. Being satisfied, or even encouraged, by catching smalls is probably one of the biggest impediments to catching quality fluke.

By mid-July, keepers become difficult to find in these waters, while sea robins and small fluke take over. By the end of the month I'm finished targeting fluke altogether in Long Island Sound, and shift my efforts to the ocean and its nearby bays. No matter what waters you call home, understanding the seasonal progression is crucial to trip planning and being able to anticipate where the quality fish will be. Let's move on to the ocean.

CHAPTER 9
BIG WATER IN AND OUT

Timing is everything is a popular saying in many aspects of life, but rarely more appropriate than when you're launching a kayak into the ocean surf. It's why I had been staring at the water for the past couple of minutes while standing next to my kayak at the ocean's edge. To someone with an untrained eye, I probably looked like I was hesitant to push out into the waves, but I was just giving myself the best chance at an uneventful start to my ocean fluke trip. I had already spent a couple of minutes deciding on the part of the beach I wanted to launch from. Some sections of the beach were bordered by a shallow sandbar where 2- to 3-foot waves built and broke in such a way that my 15-foot kayak would be tossed like a child's pool toy if I dared get close at the wrong time. While I couldn't find an ideal deeper spot to avoid these breakers entirely, I settled on an area between the bars that looked a little calmer than the rest.

The bigger waves were coming in sets of three or four, followed by long enough lulls for me to push out unscathed. "After this wave," I finally decided. Just as it collapsed into whitewater, I grabbed the bow handle and dragged the kayak into thigh-deep water. I steadied it into an oncoming wave, hopped on, and started paddling hard. It's funny how the waves always look bigger when you're sitting on the water as opposed to standing on the beach. With waves breaking on both sides, I paddled as fast as I could for the safe passage between them. Thirty seconds after stepping into the ocean I slid down the back of the last bulge and had nothing but a smooth ocean ahead. Time to fish. I wouldn't have to go far.

The sandbar that I was glad to leave in my wake was the one closest to the shore, but there were others in the 12- to 25-foot range. One was only a couple of hundred feet away. On this relatively calm day, there were no bulging or breaking waves to give its position away, but the water was clear enough that I could see the lighter colored water on top of the bar. There were enough scattered terns hitting the water to give me confidence that there was some kind of bait around. To have bait schools and pronounced bar structure was a great fluking combination, but there was a hidden factor that also helps draw fluke to this nearshore environment – bottom turbulence. Even on a calm day with a slight gentle swell, there is a lot of movement on the bottom near the sandbars. It's something I never would have appreciated without watching some of the first underwater video that I shot in the ocean. While it should be obvious that there would be bottom movement on a rough day, the video revealed little sandstorms near the 12-foot deep bar tops with only a 2-foot swell. It was interesting to see bits of debris being freed by the water movement, and there was no doubt that there was enough movement to uncover crabs and disorientate baitfish. Fluke on the other hand could just hunker down unaffected by the turbulence while snatching whatever bait washed by. Although the series of bars and troughs near the beaches of large bodies of water

 may be similar to those found in smaller sounds and bays, the wave-driven bottom turbulence is unique to this environment, and is a positive factor to consider when you're targeting fluke or other gamefish.

As I approached the bar, the water went from a light green, to tan, and then finally to dark green over the deeper water. I watched the depth on my fishfinder along the way and noted the high spot was 13 feet. When the depth leveled off at about 20 feet, I turned broadside to the gentle breeze, anticipating that it should be enough to give me a nice drift up the bar slope and would run my rig through the bottom turbulence. The nearest inlet was about a mile away, and even at that distance there was a slight influence from the rising tide and incoming inlet current.

The depth, current, and even the varied sandbar structure was very similar to what I normally fished in Long Island Sound, so the gear I used was the same. My 7-foot baitcaster rated for 10- to 20-pound-test line was ready to go with a one-ounce bucktail and a Glass Minnow teaser. I added a Gulp Swimming Mullet to each and sent it to the bottom as my drift speed stabilized at 0.7 mph. It took only a few bounces to get the first tap. A second later I converted a momentary feeling of weight to a bent rod, but the fish came up a little too easy and would be lucky to break 14 inches. Still – structure, bait, water movement, and at least some fish gave reason for optimism. The next drop produced an even smaller fish. Small brown sea robins mixed in on the high part of the bar. I set up the next drift a little farther into the deeper water, and about a hundred yards down the beach so that I would cover new bottom. My first fish was almost instantaneous, and the biggest yet, but still only around 16 inches. The 10-minute drift was nearly *lock and load* fishing and produced close to a dozen fluke, but none even close to requiring a measurement. I stuck it out for about another 45 minutes, moving down the shore for each new drift, but the result was the same nonstop action with 12- to 16-inch fluke. Although I had often done well on quality fluke on these nearshore grounds, there just didn't seem to be any size this trip. It was time for Plan B.

I could see about a half-dozen specks on the southeast horizon. I was confident these were boats working some deeper fluke grounds about a mile and a half off the beach. I had fished the area before with the kayak and even had a couple of proven GPS marks. I zoomed out my GPS plotter and headed for the marks. I was reassured to see that my heading was taking me toward the horizon specks. With a calm sea and now barely perceptible breeze, I paddled comfortably at about 4 mph. It may sound slow to a boater, but it was good enough to get me to the grounds in twenty minutes.

This was a whole new ballgame. With 70 feet of water under the yak, my first concern was how much weight I was going to need to stay near the bottom. I've never gotten away with a one-ounce jig here, so I immediately switched to a 1 1/2-ounce. The jig took long enough to get to the bottom that I had time to get a sip of water on the descent. When the spool finally stopped spinning, I disengaged the thumb bar and began jigging with more intensity than I would inshore. The more vigorous jigging would be necessary to take up any belly in the long length of line between my rod and the bottom, and keep good action on the jig. The next adjustment was mental – I had no expectation of the fast-paced action I experienced inshore. This was open and relatively uniform bottom and it lacked the pronounced edges that often concentrate inshore fish. Still, these were productive grounds, and likely benefited from the flow of the inlet that was two miles away. What this area lacked in numbers of fish, it made up for in size. My friend, Mike Mapes, could attest to that, having landed a 13.2-pounder here on the last day of the season a few years back. I would be more than happy with a 5-pounder.

As is sometimes the case, there was more of a breeze closer to shore. The wind was nearly calm here, combined with a gentle ocean current to push me along at only 0.5 mph. I bounced vigorously for a few minutes with no signs of life. While the slow drift made it possible for me to stay down with what is considered a lightweight jig in these deep waters, it didn't allow me to cover much bottom. A slow drift in an area of dispersed fish isn't a great combination, but periodic bait clouds near the bottom on the fishfinder gave me some hope that I was doing this for something other than the paddling exercise. The handful of boats in the area were more scattered than they appeared from in close, but I was encouraged to see a net go down on one about a hundred yards away and come up with a nice fish. My first hit came about five minutes in. I missed the fish once before it grabbed on for good. The first several pumps were easy before the fish made a sharp dive for the bottom. They always seem to fight harder in the deeper water, but this one was clearly larger than the fish I had been catching close to the beach. There was a little more give and take before I saw some color in the clear ocean water. The 20-incher was a welcomed sight, and I marked the spot with the GPS to give a reference point for subsequent drifts. One short fluke came up in the next five minutes of drifting.

As I paddled out to make another drift, I noted the breeze was starting to pick up. I searched around a bit and stopped on top of a deep bait school. This time it took only a few bounces to connect with a 4-pounder. By the time my jig made it to the bottom on the next drop, there was already a significant angle in the line. After twenty seconds of bouncing, I had to let more line out to get back to the bottom. Soon after that, more line was required. With the drift speed now up to 0.8

Mike Mapes and his wife Gwen with their 13.2-pound ocean fluke.

mph, and mostly wind-driven, the 1 1/2-ounce bucktail was too light to stay down. I had options to deal with this scoping. I could deploy the drift sock to cut the drift speed down, or I'd have to go to a heavier bucktail. The choice to go heavier was an easy one. The 0.8 mph drift speed was too much for the light jig in the deep water, but it was still on the slow end of the 0.5 to 1.5 mph range that I prefer. I'd rather go heavier and cover more ground in these circumstances.

I could go to two ounces, but that would only be a little better, and the rod I was using was too soft to put good action on a 2-ounce jig in deep water. I traded the inshore rod for a stiffer one that was stowed inside the hull. This 7-footer was rated for 12- to 25-pound test line and was already rigged with a 3-ounce bucktail. The 3-ounce jig stayed down beautifully. I switched from a 4-inch to a 5-inch grub on the teaser hook, hoping to tempt a larger fish with the bigger profile. Even though there's only a 1-inch difference in length, the 5-inch Gulp Swimming Mullet is much fatter and overall larger than the 4-inch. A larger profile teaser or bucktail trailer means more drag in the water, and potentially more scoping, but under these calm conditions the rig stayed down fine.

After two hours of a moderate pick of mostly 3- to 5-pound fish, the wind picked up. I managed one extra drift in the building chop by deploying the drift sock, but nearly 2 miles out on a kayak with a rising wind isn't exactly where I want to be, so I began the paddle back. With the help of the breeze on my stern, I held a steady 5 mph course and made it to the outside of the last bar in about 25 minutes. I was now faced with the part I like the least about ocean kayak fishing – landing in the surf.

The timing of this trip was favorable in that I was landing near high tide. This meant more water over the sandbars, and less building and breaking of waves. The slight wind-driven chop was of no concern, and the gentle swell was no worse than it was in the morning. Still, landing is much more difficult than launching, as the waves come in from behind you and take control. A nice feature of my Ocean Trident kayak is that I can access the inside of the hull through the large cockpit hatch. This enabled me to stow every piece of gear, including the rods and fishfinder, inside of the enclosed hull. If I flipped, I should get nothing worse than a swim in mild water. My PFD could be inflated

The kind of fluke worth paddling a mile or two into the ocean for.

if necessary. As with launching, I waited a bit outside of where the waves were breaking so that I could get a feel for the size and frequency of the larger wave sets. When I was comfortable that I knew what I was dealing with, I chose a set of larger waves that I'd follow. When the last one passed I paddled as hard as I could behind it, watching it collapse in front of me. I felt the next wave come up behind me, but it wasn't

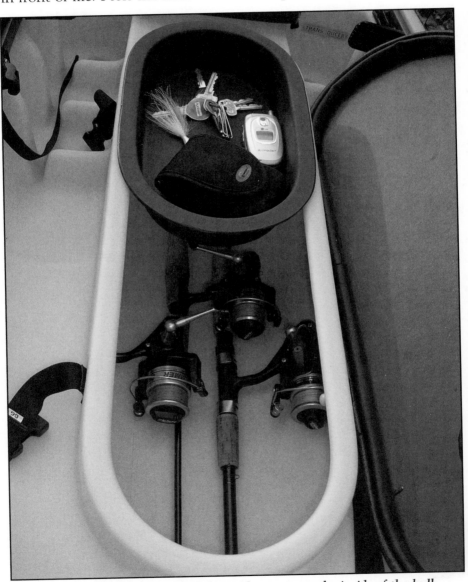

The Ocean Kayak Trident Rod Pod provides access to the inside of the hull from the cockpit. These 7-foot rods are stowed easily and safely when passing through the surf.

moving much faster than I was and I was able to keep the yak perpendicular to the wave and headed nearly straight at the beach. I surfed it
for just a few seconds before it broke, allowing me to ride the whitewater
until I came to an abrupt stop on the sand. Rather than scramble to get
out, I waited a couple of seconds for the next wave remnants, which I
used to get slightly farther up the beach. Knowing I now had almost a
full 8-second wave period before the next one hit, I hopped out and
jogged out of the wash and up the sand with a ski-tow handle that was attached to a 10-foot length of rope tied to the
bow. The line came tight just as the next wave hit and I
used it to take the yak well up the beach slope and onto
dry sand.

Using the ski rope and waiting to get out of the kayak were two
things I learned the hard way. A couple of times while landing on
earlier trips, I would land successfully, and then end up on my ass in
the wash. My first mistake was being in a hurry to get out of the kayak
while in the remnants of the wave that put me there. Inevitably that
wave was already receding, and the next one was close behind. As soon
as I stood up, the yak would get hit by the following wave. This led to
the next problem. The bow handle is slightly recessed and difficult to
grab, especially when moving. Because I was between the beach and
the kayak while trying to grab the handle, the second following wave
would push the kayak right into me. At over 15 feet long and 90
pounds geared, it had no trouble knocking me down. Waiting for the
first following wave to hit and then snatching the yak out with a rope
solved these problems.

A kayak is a surprisingly suitable craft for fishing the ocean on a
calm day. In theory, I could have used my 16-foot tin boat that I fished
out of in the previous chapter, but in practice I would never take it
through the ocean inlet, which can be downright treacherous even on
a relatively calm day. By launching and landing the kayak some
distance from the inlet currents and turbulence, I need only to deal
with the waves at the beach. The key is to choose a very calm day
when those waves are manageable. The downside of the ocean kayak
approach is that there are many days when it's too rough to get in and
out of the surf safely. It's why I found myself on my friend's 38-footer
to fish the deep water a couple of days later.

A kayak is a capable ocean fishing platform when the surf is calm.

It was a beautiful day to be on the water. The long-period 3-foot waves were barely perceptible a couple of miles off the beach, but the shore break would have been tough in a kayak. The 10-knot wind was perfect to push the boat along at around one knot. Mike throttled down in 70 feet of water, and turned the boat broadside to the breeze. In addition to the Gulp, he had some meat strips cut from fish caught the previous day. Whether these strips come from sea robins, bluefish, or legal fluke, they make great bucktail trailers and provide the added attraction of a large profile and real fish scent. I fish nothing but Gulp more than 90% of the time, but I'll tip the bucktail with a meat strip when convenient and targeting larger fish. A combination that I like for the larger ocean fluke is a meat strip on the bucktail and a 5- or 6-inch Gulp grub on the teaser hook. It's what I was dropping to the bottom as the boat stabilized for our first drift.

Watching the line angle as the rig descended, I suspected the 3-ounce bucktail was going to be too light. When the spool stopped spinning I engaged the reel and began the usual rapid jigging. I gave it about ten seconds before dropping to the bottom again to see how high the jig was riding. It took almost five seconds to touch, so it was clear that the jig was not staying near the bottom. I immediately cranked back up and traded the 3-ounce Blue Frog bucktail for a 4-ounce. This was at about the limit that my 15- to 25-pound-class baitcaster could jig effectively. The extra ounce was immediately noticeable on the next drop as it made it to the bottom faster. This time there was only a slight angle on the line when I engaged the reel and began jigging. I made it through only a few bounces before a small keeper jumped on, so I'd wait for the next drop to get a good feel for how well the jig was handling the drift.

After a minute or so had passed on the next drift without the need to drop out additional line, I was convinced that the 4-ounce was right for these conditions and the 20-pound-test braid. If it had scoped more, I would have traded the meat strip for a Gulp grub in order to try to reduce the drag. The drag of a teaser or bucktail trailer is an important consideration when trying to fight off line scope. A big meat strip hanging off a bucktail provides a great looking large-profile offering with natural scent, but it also adds bulk that creates drag and requires extra weight to stay down. The same goes for the choice of Gulp grub. The 5- and 6-inch models provide a nice large target for big ocean fluke, but also require a little additional lead to stay deep. Much of the challenge of fluking deep water requires fighting scope to keep a lively and relatively large offering near the bottom. One thing is for sure – you're unlikely to catch any fluke at all if your offering is high above their strike zone.

A couple of minutes into my second drop of the 4-ounce, I set the hook on some extra weight and the rod barely budged. A good fish for sure, but only for a second as it came off. "It will come back," I said with hopeful confidence as I immediately resumed jigging. It took only a few bounces for the fish to pounce again. The hook stuck this time. Solid runs for the bottom periodically interrupted the heavy lifts accentuated with head shakes as I worked the fish to the surface. It gave one last hard shake just before I slid it into the waiting net. The

7-plus pounder was exactly the class of fish that drove fluke anglers to these deeper waters. I had watched enough underwater video of fluke reacting to jigs to know that a fluke that hits once will almost definitely keep striking as long as the bait isn't lost. The tough meat strip on the bucktail wasn't going anywhere, and neither was the fish once it decided to eat it.

With two keepers on its first two drops, the 4-ounce bucktail would stay on my rod for the rest of the trip. Mike's outfit was a little too soft to handle 4 ounces, so he stayed with a 3-ounce. His wife, Gwen, was more comfortable with a 30-pound class outfit. There is a big difference in the line drag between 20- and 30-pound-test braid, so she used a 6-ounce Tsunami fluke ball to stay down.

The drift was steady for hours, and as is typical of this open bottom deep ocean fluking, we had a pick of quality fluke that varied with intensity. After the first two hours it was clear that a particular portion of the 20-minute drifts was producing better, so Mike shortened the drift to keep us on the best fishing. It was interesting to see how the different rigs produced during the trip.

The rapidly bounced 4-ounce rig produced the best, with 7 legal fluke to a little over 7 pounds. The largest fish was the only keeper to hit the bucktail and bait strip. The rest took the 5-inch Gulp Swimming Mullet. Gwen bounced 3 keepers to over 5 pounds on the 6-ounce fluke ball rig, with all of her keepers hitting the 5-inch Gulp teaser. There were plenty of short fluke mixed in on both rigs. Although Mike was often busy with his captain and mate duties, he still spent a fair amount of time with his rig down. Unfortunately, his baitcasting rod was a little under-powered to handle a 4-ounce bucktail, so he resorted to letting out a lot of line to stay near the bottom with a 3-ounce. He did stay in the strike zone, as was evidenced by the substantial number of short fluke and sea robins that he caught, but he didn't catch any keepers. He's an excellent fisherman, but the large angle in his line and soft rod tip made it nearly impossible for him to put a lively dancing action on the jig.

Although the breeze was gentle and the drift speed was in the perfect 1-knot range, it required a relatively heavy bucktail to stay down, even on the thin 20-pound-test braid. This was likely due to some interaction with the ocean current, which tends to be a factor in the deeper water of this particular area. It was surprising that 3 ounces was all that was required to stay down and catch the next day, despite a solid 20-knot offshore wind. It's possible the effect of the offshore wind was partially negated by the swell coming from the opposite direction. Wind speed and direction, wind waves and swells, ocean currents, and the potential of current related to a nearby inlet all affect the drift and the amount of weight required to keep an offering in the strike zone. This can be a challenge of big water fluking, and when fishing from a larger boat, you don't have the drift sock deployment option that you have in a small boat or kayak. After all, you'd probably need to drag a tent through the water to slow down a 40-footer. Some captains will resort to back-trolling to control the drift speed. This entails using the boat's engines, often alternating between slow reverse and neutral, to push the stern into the drift to slow it down. It's extra work for the captain, but can be an effective way to compensate for an unfavorable drift, or to focus the drift on a piece of productive structure. As with fluking in any environment, picking days with suitable conditions for fluke jigging is very important in ocean fishing, especially in deeper water. We fished to about 70 feet in this chapter, let's push out to deeper water on a party boat.

A 4-ounce Blue Frog bucktail and a 6-ounce Tsunami Ball Jig produced these nice ocean fluke.

CHAPTER 10
DEEP OCEAN PARTY BOAT

"Boat leaves at 7 a.m. No reservations. Just show up." It's how Captain James Foley of the *Hampton Lady* Party Boat out of Shinnecock Inlet New York ended his Facebook post that detailed the day's fishing. I had just gotten home from work and his videos of mates scrambling around the deck to net fluke in the 6- to 10-pound range was a little too much for me to take. I decided I would "just show up" the next morning.

The trip would be something new to me in that I have enough fishing opportunities on my own and others' boats that I had never fished a party boat for fluke before. I knew this one was fishing in about 85 feet of water around a 35-acre artificial reef consisting of, and I quote from the New York State Department of Conservation website: "3,000 tires in 3-tire units; 3 barges; a tug; a wood drydock; 2 wood boats; a steel cruiser; a steel and concrete tower; 2 steel trawlers; surplus armored vehicles; steel and concrete bridge rubble; and 2,400 tons of jetty stone." Captain Jim's extensive experience fishing the reef earned him a well-deserved reputation for putting his clients on big fluke.

I watched the captain's videos carefully and took note of the gear most people were using. The rods were all significantly heavier than the ones I used for fluke. Between the depth, current, structure, size of the fish, and the way the big boat drifted, I was concerned that my baitcasting outfits and associated bucktails wouldn't cut it. I emailed a local tackle shop contact familiar with that boat and he said most anglers used chicken rigs with 4 to 12 ounces of weight. That was consistent with the moderate to heavy action rods I saw in the video.

My first mistake in preparing for the trip was in not anticipating that the boat supplied sinkers, so that certainly added weight to the gear bag that I assembled. One type of chicken rig is simply a sinker loop at the bottom and a couple of dropper loops above for hooks. My plan was to show up at the boat at 5:30 a.m. with the material to tie rigs, figure out what I needed, and then tie some while I was waiting. I would bring my usual bucktail leaders, bucktails, and fluke balls that I used on Mike's boat, along with plenty of Gulp. My main rod was a medium power 30-pound-class 7-footer with a Penn Levelwind reel spooled with 30-pound-test braid. It would handle 6 ounces comfortably, but could go heavier if needed. Given a forecast of winds less than 10 knots, I didn't anticipate having to worry about going up to 10 or 12 ounces. As many party boat anglers do, I would bring a second rod, but wasn't sure whether to go heavier or lighter than the 30-pound class outfit. The solution was simple. I'd put both in the truck and then choose the spare rod based on what everybody else had.

I pulled into the empty parking lot ninety minutes before the scheduled departure and thought for a minute I must be in the wrong place. My only party boat experience was for Montauk-based cod fishing in which anglers routinely showed up several hours before the boat sailed. With a single rod I walked down the dock to find a completely empty *Hampton Lady*. I had my pick of spots. When I had watched the video from the previous day I noted that the action was on the Starboard side, so I settled on the Starboard corner stern.

I went back to my truck for the rest of the gear, and chose a heavier rod for my spare. Within 15 minutes a steady stream of patrons made their way to the boat, and I struck up a few conversations and inspected some rod rigging to learn what to tie and expect. I heard things like "minimum 6 ounces" and "heavy bucktails don't work out there." I proceeded to tie a few chicken rigs with 30-pound-test Fluorocarbon for my 30-pound-class outfit. With about 45 minutes left before departure, I made another survey of rods around the boat, and noted a few lighter than my main rod, and almost nothing heavier. I returned to the truck to swap my heavier spare for my 15- to 25-pound-class baitcaster, which was already rigged with a 3-ounce bucktail.

A version of a chicken rig.

If I had any hopes of using that rod, they were dashed on the three-mile ride out when the mate who was passing out the boat-supplied sinkers handed me an 8-ounce. I thanked him and asked if I could also have a 6, which he gladly dug out of his lead bucket. Besides the sinkers, this boat provided a superb assortment of high quality baits. They had squid, spearing, various fish strips, and even Gulp. My first drop would be with a pair of 5-inch Gulp grubs on 3/0 hooks adorned with Tsunami Hollow Teasers. This would offer the fluke some high visibility and large profile targets. With all of the anticipation that goes with the start of a fishing trip, I disengaged the clutch on my reel and sent the rig to the bottom when the boat's horn sounded. While waiting for the rig to make it to the bottom, I noted the conditions were beautiful, with a gentle 5- to 10-knot onshore breeze. When the rig touched down I did my best to impart my usual rapid jigging action, but it was much more difficult to accomplish with the heavier gear. I kept at it anyway, hoping to make my rig stand out among the others. I had nothing to show for the first five minutes, but noted that scoping was not an issue with the 6-ounce sinker. On one of the lifts I was excited to feel some extra weight and set the hook immediately. I was disappointed the fish came up so easily, as the 16-incher was not what I was out there for. The next fish wasn't much better. I swapped one of

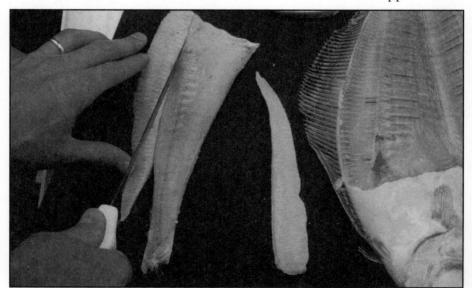

Fin strips make excellent baits. Some State regulations require that you retain the fluke carcass from which the strips were cut. The carcass counts against the bag limit.

the Gulp grubs for a boat-supplied strip of fluke, but that offering made no difference.

In the first two hours I saw a few scattered keeper fluke come up, but nothing big. I was tiring from trying to vigorously jig the boat rod when the angler next to me hooked up a nice fish. The turning point of my trip came when I saw what looked like a 3-ounce bucktail hanging out of the mouth of the 7-pounder. I immediately cranked up and swapped the boat rod for my baitcaster and sent the rig to the bottom with a pair of Gulp grubs. The rig stayed down nicely, and within a minute I set the hook on my first quality fluke. Bringing the fish up

A nice party boat fluke that pounced on a 3-ounce Blue Frog Deep Diver bucktail tipped with a fluke strip.

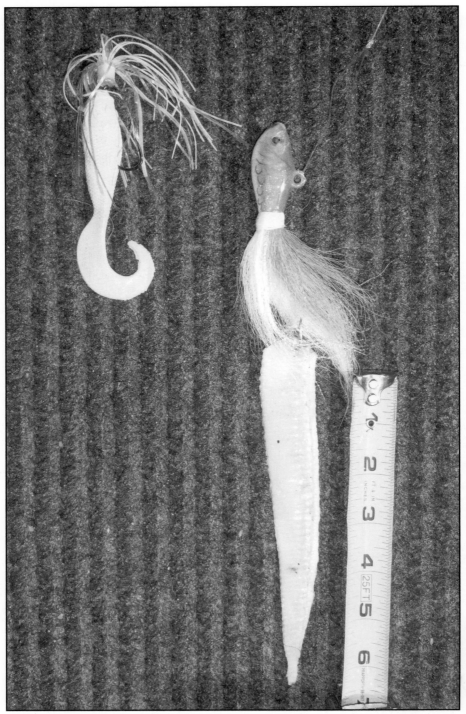

A 5-inch Gulp Swimming Mullet with a Tsunami Holo Teaser on top of a 3-ounce Blue Frog bucktail tipped with a fluke strip.

from 85 feet on the baitcaster was fun and tested the drag. It was a good feeling to slide the 5-pounder into the net, but there were better fish ahead.

The next twenty minutes were quiet for me. Being new to the boat, I was keeping an eye on the other anglers to see what was working. When I saw an angler on the Port side land his second quality fluke, I noticed he also had a bucktail on, but his was tipped with a meat strip. As we ran up for the next drift, I traded the Gulp grub on the bucktail for a meat strip. This made a big difference as I boated two keepers on the next drift, including a 7-pounder. The fishing had not improved much for the anglers around me, but I felt like I now had the hot hand. I boated a 4-pounder and a couple of shorts on the next drift, and was amazed that my cooler was now looking pretty good, when not long before I was still trying to get it dirty.

With one fish to go to make my five fish limit, I sent my rig on its long trip to the bottom. I jigged vigorously, convinced that the rapid bouncing was causing my rig to stand out and attract attention. My rig was down less than a minute when I missed a sharp grab. A few seconds later I doubled the rod over briefly, but then nothing. I kept it bouncing not wanting to lose the fish's interest. The third time was the charm as I stuck the fish hard and a tough battle commenced. It put up a lot of resistance for the first fifteen feet or so, and then went back to the bottom on a strong run. As I worked to get the line back, I detected that awful feeling of something rubbing against my line. I was pretty sure I was too high to be against the structure, and realized a line from a few anglers up the boat had drifted back and caught mine. I asked for some slack, and he gave it. Worried that his rig might fray my taut line, I took it a little slower on this fish. As it was coming up, the other angler's line surfaced with a hook riding my main line. The mate made a move to unhook it, but I asked that he just leave it and let it slide on the line. I was more concerned about giving the fish slack. The other angler held steady and I kept the fish moving all the way to the waiting net. The nearly 8-pounder was a nice way to cap off my limit.

My timing couldn't have been better, as the breeze was picking up. The small whitecaps on the ride up for the next drift convinced me to go to a 4-ounce bucktail. That was good enough to stay down through the next drift, which produced several fish near the legal size limit for me, including a double-header. The captain was alternating the orientation of the boat on each drift, meaning if your line was pointing away from the boat on one drift, it would be going under the boat on the next. With a building chop, my second drift with the 4-ounce bucktail was one in which my line was heading under the boat. When I realized I needed to keep letting line out to stay near the bottom, I cranked up so that I wouldn't hook any lines on the opposite side of the boat. I then went back to my heavier boat rod and the 8-ounce sinker that the mate had handed me on the way out. I didn't even bother trying 6 ounces, realizing that 6 ounces with a 30-pound-test main line was not going to stay down any better than 4 ounces on 20-pound-test. I stayed with the 8-ounce rig and heavier outfit for the rest of the trip. It produced a fair number of fluke, but nothing close to the size of the fish that fell to the rapidly bounced bucktail on the baitcaster.

While I watched other anglers on this trip to see what was working best, I also noted what wasn't working. As I had observed on some other ocean trips, the worst thing that you could do was drag a bait along the bottom. An angler near me was using a traditional bottom rig with various combinations of squid, bait strips, and spearing. He caught no keepers. Another angler ran bait combos on a 3-foot leader from a 6-ounce fluke ball, which he bounced slowly on the bottom. He caught one keeper. Both of these anglers caught a lot of skates. I would have never known those skates were there from my jigging efforts. Given a skate's mouth is on the underside of the fish, they aren't very well designed to snatch a moving jig from a couple of feet off the bottom.

I got a good tip from an angler I chatted with on the way out – "Stay away from the squid and spearing if you're focused on fluke." The reason was that there were also a lot of sea bass around. These are excellent eating fish and were very worthy of targeting on this trip, as they were plentiful around the reef structure. Some anglers did target them and managed some nice fillets. The problem was that there were also a lot of undersized sea bass. I viewed cranking these to the surface as lost valuable time, and many times they just cleaned the bait off the hooks. I was definitely willing to trade the sea bass action for bottom time that I could use to tempt fluke. The advice was right on the money. The squid and spearing anglers were almost constantly cranking mostly short sea bass, while I caught only one on a Gulp grub. Fortunately the sea bass were not shredding the Gulp baits on this trip, as they sometimes do. If that had been the case, I would have fished meat strips instead.

The big boat seemed to magnify the usual up and down motion that you'll feel when fishing a large body of water. The ocean is rarely perfectly flat, as is often the case on bay or sound waters. Instead, there's a constant vertical motion with the waves, even on a relatively calm day. No matter the size of the craft, this means the angler needs to pay careful attention to staying in contact with the jig while going up and down. Although I sometimes use 6-foot rods in my kayak, I prefer the longer 7-foot rod on the ocean because it helps me keep contact with the rig. While the feeling of slack on the line when fishing flat water signals a hit, on the ocean it often means the boat has

A pair of 10-pound class pool contenders.

dropped and introduced that slack. Paying close attention to stay in contact will help you maintain good action on the jig. The vertical displacement of the boat on the waves also affects hooksets. If you're setting the hook while the boat is dropping, the slack created by the drop of the boat will absorb much of the energy of your hookset. Keep this in mind and set hard and be sure to put a sharp bend in the rod. Finally, the up and down motion should be considered when you're reeling a fish to the surface. If the boat drops and reduces pressure on the fish, it could slide off the hook. On the flip side if a fish dives while the boat is going up, your drag better be set appropriately to keep the line from breaking.

In order to winch decent fish from deep water on my small baitcasting outfit, I needed to pump the rod. While cranking fish up, one of the mates cautioned me about this, and urged me to just crank steadily. Although the small reel was matched well to the rod and line strength, I couldn't rely solely on its gears to gain line. It's certainly OK, and in some cases necessary, to pump a rod while reeling up a fish. You just need to be careful not to put any slack in the line when you drop your rod to take a few cranks. As long as you keep a bend in the rod, you should have no worries that the hook is going to slide out of the fish.

Something I can't stress enough is that even though this book is dedicated to relatively light tackle jigging, there are scenarios in which the light tackle approach simply will not work. During the last hour of this party boat trip the drift was too fast to fish deep water without at least 8 ounces of lead. The fishing was still productive at this time, but there was no way to stay down without a heavy weight. Fishing a half-pound weight requires a rod with enough backbone to jig it, and that rod will require an appropriately matched reel and heavier line. No matter what tackle is required to handle the conditions, the objective should still be the same – bounce the rig vigorously near the bottom. If you have to go to 8 ounces, I'd suggest something like an 8-ounce Blue Frog Deep Diver or SPRO bucktail, or a Tsunami Ball Jig Lure, AKA fluke ball. All of these lures are made for deep water fluke fishing and carry hooks of the appropriate size for these fish.

I prefer baitcasting tackle because I feel it gives more convenient depth control, but many anglers do just fine with spinning tackle. Elias Vaisberg, a kayak fishing guide who frequently fishes deep water in the

New York Bight, told me he prefers spinning gear because he feels he can get his rig to the bottom faster than with a conventional reel. He believes that when you open the bail on a spinning reel, the line falls off the reel with less resistance than with a revolving spool reel. This is a good point, but may depend on reel performance. As their name implies, baitcasting reels are made for casting, so it takes very little pressure to rotate the spool. I did notice at least one angler with spinning gear on the party boat trip do quite well jigging bucktails. A few weeks later on a very calm day, a Hampton Lady patron used an 8- to 17-pound class spinning rod and a 1 1/2-ounce bucktail to pull three doormats between 10 and 11.25 pounds from the 85-foot depths. Whether you choose spinning or baitcasting gear, the important thing is that it's spooled with thin braided line, preferably in the 15- to 20-pound-test range.

Even though I can cover a lot of water with my kayak and boat, the deep water ocean fluke grounds fished by the Hampton Lady were a little out of my normal range. It was nice to be able to just show up and box a cooler of big fluke despite my lack of experience with that boat. If you're fishing a party boat for the first time, it's best to start by learning what you can from the mates, captain, and other anglers. It's also important to have confidence in what you already know. I had a great trip, but would have done even better if had I fished my usual baitcasting gear and technique from the start. That was definitely the way to go before the wind picked up, but I needed to switch to what others had recommended once the drift speed increased. One of the beauties of party boat fishing is that for a nominal fee, anyone can get in on the action targeting numerous species in many regions. If you're looking to expand your fluke fishing horizons, a party boat trip can be an inexpensive and productive way to go.

CHAPTER 11
DOORMAT PURSUIT

As the party boat trip came to a close, I couldn't help but look at the shoreline and think about how I could fish the reef area with my kayak. At 2.7 miles out from the beach, it would be a long paddle for sure. If I planned my trips properly, I could paddle out with the help of outgoing inlet current and return with the aid of incoming. As these trips would be executed only under very calm conditions, I estimated a leisurely paddling speed at a little over 4 mph. This translated to an approximate 40-minute paddle each way – long, but doable. Using a combination of NOAA and surfing websites, I watched the wind and wave forecasts carefully and chose a day with predicted 5-knot winds, 2-foot seas, and the appropriate inlet currents to assist my paddling efforts.

The morning air was still and comfortably cool as I readied my kayak at the ocean's edge on the west side of the inlet. Other than stowing a few extra pounds of 2- to 6-ounce bucktails inside the hull, I was geared the same as I would be for any ocean trip. The launch point was chosen carefully. With the marine weather buoys indicating a 2.5-foot swell from the southeast, I was counting on the inlet's west jetty to intercept the waves and provide me with a sheltered launching and landing point. I had gotten this part of the trip right. Only small waves snuck into the pocket formed by the intersection of the jetty and the beach. No wave timing was necessary as I pulled the kayak into thigh-deep water, hopped on, and paddled away uneventfully. I paced myself, and was content with the fairly steady 4.2 mph reading on my GPS. Slightly less than 40 minutes after leaving the beach, I approached the group of around 15 boats fishing the reef.

Now what? There's a big difference between going out on someone else's boat and relying on their experience and expertise to put you on fish, and having to figure out an entirely new area on your own. I understood that if I had just stayed in the bay and fished the areas I was familiar with, I'd probably have a couple of keepers in the cooler bag by now, but I wasn't after just keepers. My goal was to put a 10-pound fluke in the kayak. If I caught it on this trip, I would understand that it was just a lucky catch. My objectives for this trip were to learn a little about the structure, catch a few nice fluke, and hopefully put a couple of fish-proven sets of coordinates into my GPS that I could leverage on subsequent trips. The kayak 10-pound goal was one that I set for the summer season in which I hoped to make several kayak trips to the reef.

For now, I was clueless and I knew it. With 35 acres of man-made reef structure, I had no idea where to start. An observation I made on the party boat trip was that the captain must have been avoiding the heaviest structure, because over the course of the entire day, I saw only one angler snag bottom briefly. As I entered the loose collection of boats, the fishfinder lit up with a mess of reef clutter and I made sure to keep paddling until I was past the most jagged parts of it. The next thing I looked for was a little bit of space where I wouldn't be very close to the other boats, which generally ranged from 20- to 40-footers.

I finally stopped paddling when I found a suitable opening. My next decision was one of the most important in fluke jigging – choosing the bucktail weight. There was no wind and the surface of the water was glassy. Wanting to always fish with the lightest weight jig possible, I chose a 2-ounce chrome pink SPRO. With 83 feet of water under the kayak, I knew 2 ounces would be on the light end of the appropriate range. I had some previously frozen meat strips with me, and put one of these on the bucktail and added a 6-inch Gulp Grub to my Tsunami Holo Teaser hook.

I sent the rig on its long trip to the bottom and began bouncing it vigorously when it got there. I immediately went into assessment mode watching the angle of my line and hitting the reel's thumb bar a few times in the first minute to confirm that the bucktail was heavy enough to stay near the bottom without scoping out. The first hookup came about 5 minutes into the drift, and the weight on the rod combined with the unmistakable fluke head shakes had me thinking I was already into a quality fluke. My first glimpse of color under the kayak looked unusual until a few more cranks cleared up the mystery. There was a near 15-inch sea bass on the Gulp, and a roughly 20-inch fluke on the bucktail. Before I could even reach for the net, the fluke came off and I was left with just a barely short sea bass. Still, this was good enough to mark the spot as a point of reference on the GPS. I would never have guessed that it would be the only mark I would need for the rest of this trip and most of the next.

The drift was slow, less than 0.5 mph, but it was enough to cover some bottom. I paddled through the GPS mark on my way to make another drift and noticed a little bit of clutter on the bottom, but nothing as drastic as the main reef. I set up just slightly up-drift of the mark. As I drifted slowly along, I was struck by how dead quiet it was, despite the presence of the other boats in the area. Looking around it was clear that there just wasn't much going on to make noise about. I kept jigging vigorously, hoping to attract and trigger whatever fluke were around.

I hesitated just slightly at a questionable feeling of extra weight on the line, and then buried the hook hard. There was no doubt that I had just stuck a quality ocean fluke. After a little give and take, line went onto the small baitcaster steadily as I looked at the plotter to see that I was almost right on top of my GPS mark. The evening before the trip, I cut the handle on a large landing net to a manageable size for the kayak. I was glad to have the extra-wide opening as I slid the 7-pounder in. Since none of the other boats seemed to be doing much, and I had caught a couple of fish without snagging bottom, I was on my way to being married to this GPS mark for the rest of the trip. Given that I couldn't cover much ground with the slow drift, and I had no idea where else I should be trying, it seemed wise to just stay on what was working.

That GPS mark and the 7-pounder were the two best takeaways of the trip. I caught four more keepers averaging around 20 inches over the next 90 minutes, but added only one more in the following two hours. I took note that all six keepers chose the Gulp-tipped Holo Teaser over the bucktail with the meat strip trailer. This was exactly the opposite of how things played out for me on the party boat trip. One of the pleasant surprises was how comfortable it was fishing in the kayak among the larger boats. It seemed the whole reef crowd respected some sort of etiquette in that no one was racing between spots. I left

Note the safety flag for increased visibility for other boaters. The Canyon brand cooler bag behind the seat holds the day's catch.

realizing that I had to deal with more and larger boat waves fishing near the bay channels than I did sitting out on the reef. I'd be back the next time the conditions permitted. That day came two weeks later.

I ran the same play launching early into the jetty pocket and using the push of the ebb current to help me out to the reef. I was happy to have my GPS mark as a proven starting point, and felt more comfortable easing into the group of larger boats this time. I also made a slight tweak to the rig. I normally use a 3/0 Gamakatsu Baitholder for the teaser hook, but this time went up to a 5/0. The 3/0 is a perfect fit for the smaller Gulp baits, and does work well with the larger ones. I reasoned that the much thicker 6-inch grubs would fit better on a hook with a longer shank and wider gap. Besides, the fish I was interested in would have no trouble with the larger hook.

It didn't take long to put the first two respectable keepers in the yak. As with the previous trip, both hit the Gulp. It was time to make a change. Along with the usual Gulp Grubs and Swimming Mullets, I had brought along a couple of packages of green 6.5-inch Gulp Nemesis baits. I replaced the meat strip on the bucktail with one of these and was amazed at the seductive long undulating action it had when dragged through the water. It spent less than a minute bouncing the bottom before it was engulfed by a fluke pushing 7 pounds.

The trip went very much like the previous one. When noon came, I was almost ready to head in when I saw Mike and Gwen's boat entering the fleet. I told them I had done well with 6 keepers and a pair of nice sea bass, and they cruised up-drift to fish the same general area I had been working. With moderate cloud cover, comfortable temperatures, and a flat ocean, I decided it was a little too nice to stop fishing.

I landed fish of 5 and 6 pounds on the next two drifts. Mike's boat was close enough on one of the fish that I was able to paddle over for a picture. About halfway through my next drift I saw Mike's boat cruising slowly in my direction. I jokingly thought to myself that he probably wanted a picture of a 10-pounder. The joke was over when he held up a 10-pound fluke. I noted his drift had been just slightly, maybe a hundred feet, inside of mine. After getting a couple of pictures of Mike's doormat, we both headed back up to the top of the drift. He was

Mike and Gwen with their 10-pound fluke caught light tackle bucktailing in 80 feet of water.

already a couple of minutes into his drift when I started mine. A few minutes later I heard some commotion near his boat and looked back in time to see him net a 9-pounder. Two doormats in two drifts. My 5- to 7-pounders seemed underwhelming now.

I quickly pulled up my line and headed in slightly to what I believed was a position immediately up-drift of where he hooked the second big one, and then hit the "mark" button on my GPS. When I glanced at the jagged bottom line of the fishfinder, I realized I must have moved in a little too far, as I was now over the reef. I moved back out slowly until the fishfinder indicated I had cleared the structure. The GPS mark I had just taken would serve as a good reference point for the outer edge of the reef, and the 200-foot stretch between it and my original GPS mark would define a productive slice of water for subsequent drifts. Unfortunately, it didn't work out that way. My attempt to reproduce Mike's drift tanked my fishing, as I caught next to nothing over the next hour. I finally gave up and started the long paddle back to shore.

It had been a great trip by all measures, but I couldn't help but wonder what might have been if my drift lines had been 100 feet to the north. I learned from Mike the next day that his fish were all caught over clean bottom, and the one time they did hit the structure they hung up and lost a rig. The 5/0 hooks that I used on this trip worked out well and I lost very few grubs, which may have been due to the longer hook shank. When I traded the meat strip for the Gulp Nemesis on the bucktail, that part of the rig came to life and produced fish throughout the trip.

I would have to wait a week to get another crack at it. This trip was pushed later into the morning to coincide with the tides. I had a flat ocean and forecasted 5-knot winds, but I wouldn't leave the beach until after 9 a.m., near slack incoming current. I would return near slack outgoing. If the drift direction permitted, I planned to focus on the slice of water between my two GPS marks, and be a little less shy about fishing close to the main reef.

I stopped paddling when I reached my original outer GPS mark and rigged up the rod with a 2-ounce bucktail tipped with a meat strip along with a 6-inch Gulp Grub on the 5/0 Holo Teaser hook. The movement of the kayak while I was rigging up gave me a good indication of my drift speed (0.5 mph) and direction (inshore). With this information I paddled slightly outside of the mark to start my first drift, and was pleased that the plotter showed me drifting directly toward my second GPS mark. It didn't take long before I put a 20-incher in the cooler bag. In a few more minutes, I added a second one about the same size. The next two drops quickly produced a small keeper and a short. The plotter indicated that my drift had stayed steady, and I was now just outside of the GPS mark on the edge of the reef. I decided to keep jigging until I saw dense structure on the fishfinder, realizing that my odds of snagging bottom increased with every second I left the rig down.

Between the fast-paced bite and the impending structure, I anticipated that I would feel something very soon. The instant I did, I set the hook fast and hard, but the heavily bent rod didn't budge. "Stuck" was what went through my mind for a split-second, before I felt and saw the rod tip bouncing against what otherwise felt like a cement block. With effort, I put several pumps of line onto the reel before the fish pulled the rod tip into the water and took back most of the line. The fish barely budged from the end of this run, but with effort I gained some more line. Again, the rod tip was pulled into the water as the drag gave up line. The next minute was spent lifting and cranking down hard to put line on the reel while being sure to keep a bend in the rod. At this point I knew if I didn't have something unexpected, like a foul-hooked fish, this could be what I was looking for. At first sight I immediately noted the bright green grub in the mouth area, and then the size. Two more pumps of the rod, and I reached for the net. It was carelessly tangled, but I calmly gave it a couple of shakes to straighten it out with one arm while I put the fish on an approach course with the other. They came together almost perfectly into an explosion of water. With the ring of the net above the water, and the doormat secure in the deep mesh below, I held it there for a few seconds before lifting it into the kayak. I was soaked from the thrashing.

I generally plan well, and this was no exception. I knew from the start that I would not keep a fish this size. I was in no need of additional fluke fillets, and the fish was clearly too big for my cooler bag. I did want a weight, but I didn't want the fish thrashing around while hanging from its gill plate. I came prepared with a solution. I reached behind me and pulled out a large mesh bag that I had brought along for just this occasion. I put the mesh bag on my scale and zeroed it. Then, I removed the bag from the scale, put it inside the landing net, and put the fish in the mesh bag while everything was still in the landing net. Now I needed only to hang the mesh bag on the scale as it cradled the fish. Double digits! It wasn't by much, as the scale reading fluctuated at a couple of ounces over 10 pounds.

I carefully removed the fish from the mesh bag and placed it over the side while holding onto its tail. I held onto it for about 10 seconds to revive it a little, and when I felt it kick, I knew it was ready to go. I hoped to watch it swim away, but it went directly under the kayak instead, and out of sight. Mission accomplished.

CHAPTER 12
MAKING FLUKE BUCKTAILS

From 1/2-ounce back bay jigs that dart across the shallows, to 8-ounce jigs capable of staying in the strike zone in deep ocean waters, well-equipped fluke anglers need a variety of different weight bucktails to match the varied situations. If you fish frequently over obstruction-cluttered bottoms or often encounter toothy predators such as bluefish, your supply will need to be pretty deep to make it through a season. At an average cost of $4 to $8 each depending on weight, a season's bucktail tab can get expensive in a hurry. Home production is a nice way to help pass the off-season, while saving substantial money and building an arsenal of bucktails of superior quality. It's not just about saving money. Tying your own bucktails gives you a level of customization and flexibility that can be attained only by doing it yourself.

Besides the long-term cost savings achievable by pouring your own heads, you'll also have some flexibility in hook sizes and styles. Mold manufacturers will recommend specific brand, style, and hook size for each head, but you should feel free to experiment. The ability to use my preferred size and style of hooks was the reason I began making my own fluke bucktails. With few exceptions, such as the bucktails made by the manufacturers mentioned in Chapter 2, most commercially available bucktails weighing 2 ounces or more do not have proper hooks for fluke fishing.

All of my fluke bucktail heads are made with *Ultra Minnow Jig* molds from the *Do-It* corporation. You can browse the full array of Do-It ds at www.do-itmolds.com, and many local tackle outlets carry their products. At the time of this writing, they were making four Ultra Minnow Jig molds. Three of those collectively produced ten different weight jigs in the 1/2- to 8-ounce range. Much of my fluke fishing, especially from shore, is done with 3/4, 1, and 1 1/2-ounce jigs. I ignore Do-It's hook brand and size recommendations and use Gamakatsu style 604 hooks in sizes 4/0 through 7/0 for the mold that makes 1/2, 3/4, 1, and 1 1/2-ounce jigs. Those hooks may sound big for fluke, but it's due only to the way Gamakatsu sizes their jig hooks.

Figure 1

Beyond this weight range is where fluke anglers looking to make their own jigs start running into trouble. The next size Ultra Minnow jig mold is a good example why. This mold makes 2, 3, and 4-ounce jigs all designed to carry an 8/0 Mustad 34184 hook. That is exactly the hook that I use for bucktailing large stripers in ocean inlets, but it is not a hook that I would consider using for fluke. The solution to this problem is not as simple as substituting different jig hooks because, as far as I can tell, no one sells a jig hook that fits these molds with a hook gap and style appropriate for fluke. I work around this problem by using a #2 brass sinker eye for the jig eye, and then placing an 8/0 Gamakatsu 604 jig hook in the hook slot. Figures 1 and 2 show how these components fit in the mold. This gives me my favorite style fluke jigging hook in jigs up to 4 ounces.

Figure 2

Moving up to the next Ultra Minnow mold that makes 5, 6, and 8-ounce jigs, you'll find it's cut for even larger 9/0 Mustad 34184 hooks. Again, I use a #2 brass sinker eye for the jig eye. Tapping the brass eye in a little grease before placing it in the mold will help keep it in place. I still prefer the 8/0 Gamakatsu 604 hooks for this mold, but because these 5- to 8-ounce jigs are often fished on heavier line and rods, some anglers might prefer a stronger hook. Mustad 34184 jig hooks in 5/0 and 6/0 sizes are good options.

The beauty of substituting a sinker eye for the hook eye is that the choice of jig hooks is expanded greatly and the angler can carefully tailor hook gap, length, and thickness to the particular applications those jigs are likely to see. For example, I would be more concerned with hook strength if I knew I would have to wrestle fish from the edge of a wreck as opposed to working them to the surface over open bottom. It's this level of potential customization that provides benefits well beyond the economics of self-production.

I prefer an electric *Hot Pot II* for melting lead. Just plug it in, and it melts 4 pounds of lead in about 10 minutes. Since it is set up to pour the lead into molds directly from the pot, no ladle is required. Good sources to buy lead at a reasonable price are scrap yards and tire shops.

Melting lead is serious business that can lead to injury if you're not careful. I always do my lead pouring outdoors to avoid the fumes. You don't need anything better than a precipitation-free day warmer than about 35 degrees. Minimize exposed skin to the greatest extent possible. Long sleeves, gloves, a brimmed hat, and protective eyewear are all called for. Be very careful when putting solid lead into the molten pot. I use a long pair of tongs to further distance myself from danger. Introducing any significant moisture into the hot lead can be disastrous, since it can splatter for quite some distance. Keep the kids away. You don't want them breathing the fumes or knocking anything over. Work in an uncluttered area to minimize the chance of an accident.

Metal molds need to be kept hot while in use in order to work properly. Before I attempt the first jig of a pouring session with a metal mold, I fill all of the cavities with hot lead and let the mold sit for a minute or so. I leave my Hot Pot plugged in constantly, and give the molten lead time to heat up thoroughly when I add sizable pieces of

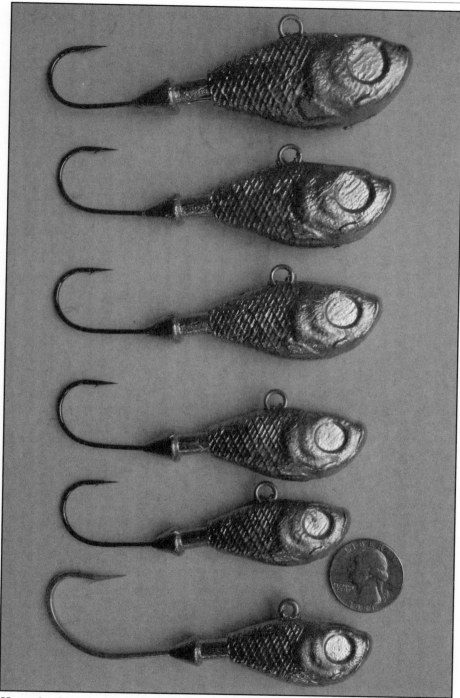

Heavy bucktail heads in the 3- to 8-ounce range with Gamakatsu jig hooks of the appropriate size for fluke fishing. Note the bottom head has the factory-recommended 8/0 hook, which is too large for most fluke fishing applications.

lead. If the lead and/or the mold are not hot enough, the jig collars (where the hair is tied) may not form properly. If a jig doesn't come out correctly, you can simply dip it into the molten lead to melt off the malformed head, carefully tap off the remaining lead on the hook, then reuse the hook.

I always pour one jig at a time, even though each mold has at least three cavities. I do this because it's easier to position the hook properly if I hold the hook with one hand and close the mold with the other. Pour the lead into the mold in a steady fashion until some comes out of the top. It takes only a few seconds for the jig to solidify enough for it to be ready to be removed from the mold. I place my hot finished jig heads on a sheet of plywood to cool. After cooling, I use a pair of pliers to remove the excess lead nugget from the jig head. A simple twist usually does the trick.

I paint all of my jig heads with *Pro-Tec Powder Paint*. Once you get the hang of using it, painting is easy, inexpensive, and the finished product will be very durable. To apply the paint, hold the jig by the hook bend and heat the head thoroughly and evenly over a propane torch (Figure 4). Plunge the head into the powder for about a second, and then firmly tap off the excess by banging the jig on the edge of the container (Figure 5). At this point, the jig should look like it's been dipped in wet paint. It can now be hung up to cool. Use a nail to stir and fluff up the powder after every couple of jigs.

In order to get the hardest possible paint finish, cure the paint at about 300 degrees for 25 minutes. I simply heat the kitchen oven to that temperature and hang the previously painted jigs from the oven racks. Be careful not to heat the heads much higher than 300 degrees, because it can damage some hook finishes. The temperature needs to be hot enough for the paint to become tacky.

Nicely cleaned and preserved deer tails in various colors can be purchased from bait and tackle shops, as well as from mail-order outlets. They typically cost between $5 and $7 each, and are responsible for most of the cost of homemade bucktail jig production. All of my deer tails are freebies that are donated by hunters. Most jig makers that I know would take such tails, cut the bone out, and salt them. I simply hose them down thoroughly, and then lay them out on a newspaper

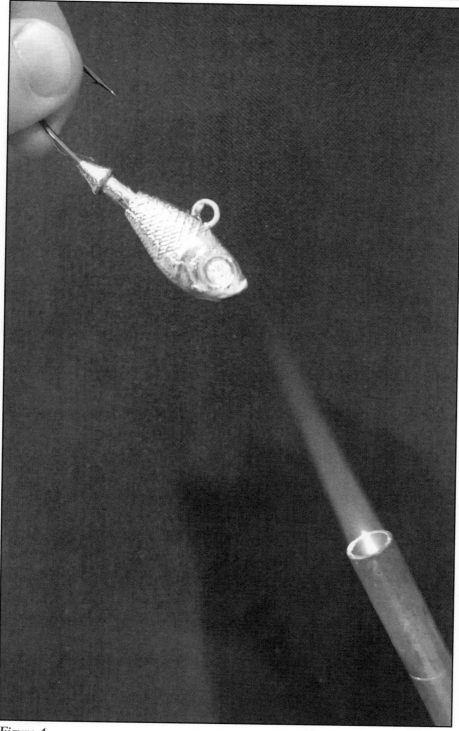

Figure 4

Figure 5

covered plywood board in my garage for a few weeks. After they've dried, I pack them into 2-gallon Ziploc freezer bags (about eight to a bag), and store them away in my basement. I've stored deer tails in this fashion for as long as 15 years without any problems.

Using a pair of sharp scissors, I cut off all of the usable white hair and place it in small piles. Each pile will hold about one-third of the total amount of hair that will go on each jig. The longer hairs will be saved for the larger jigs. The number of jigs that you'll be able to tie from an average deer tail will vary with the jig weight, but you should get at least six when tying the heaviest jigs, and possibly double that with light-weight jigs. When I tie jigs for striper fishing, I don't use the brown hair because most of it isn't long enough for the long shank hooks that I use in those jigs. The brown hair is however long enough for the 1/2- to 1 1/2-ounce fluke jigs. Because fluke often feed on brown colored crustaceans such as crabs and shrimp, it makes sense to use the brown hair to make small brown jigs. If you use the brown hair, it's not unreasonable to get as many as 15 small jigs from a single deer tail, which makes tying your own bucktails quite cost-effective.

Most people who tie bucktails use a vise, but I'm quite comfortable working without one and have been doing it that way for a long time. I wrap a single layer of size D rod winding thread across the jig collar, then *lightly* and one at a time wrap three hair piles onto the jig (Figure 6). Since the thread is still somewhat loose, it is now easy to evenly disperse the hair around the jig (Figure 7). At this point, I start wrapping the jig tightly to secure the hair. With the hair in place firmly, but the wrap still incomplete, I use a box cutter to trim the excess hair where the collar meets the rest of the jig head (Figure 8). After trimming, the tight wrapping resumes until it's almost complete. I then lay a pre-cut loop of thread on the wrap and make a few winds over it. The main thread is then cut, placed into the loop, and pulled under the final wraps so that the threads will not unravel (Figure 9). Cut the loose end off, and you're done tying. The wraps are then secured with epoxy.

Even if you have no interest in making bucktails from scratch, the latter steps in the procedure can be used to rehab worn out store-bought

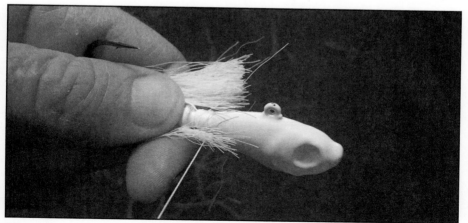

Figure 6

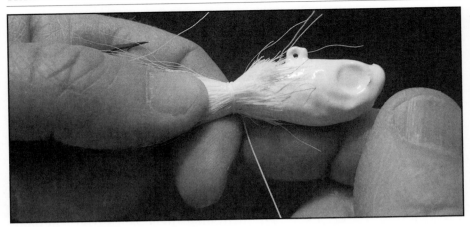

Figure 7

Figure 8

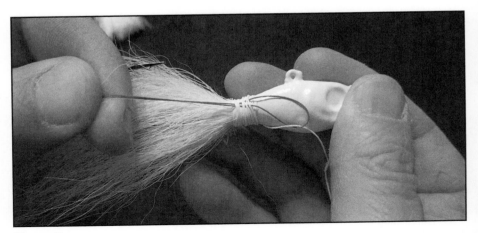

Figure 9

bucktails that have had their hair thinned out by fish. No matter how well-tied your bucktails are, fluke have substantial teeth that eventually trim the hair down to the point that your once pretty bucktail ends up as little more than a painted jighead. By purchasing a deer tail or two and some thread, you can bring these back to life.

As mentioned, I'm fine with using nothing but white jigs for fluke, and maybe some brown when the fish are on crabs. If you want to experiment with different colors, you can follow these instructions that I use for tying the wine red bucktails that I favor for striper fishing at night. I tie all of my jigs with white hair and thread, then dye completed jigs to desired colors using RIT powder dye that is commonly found in grocery and department stores. Before dyeing, I soak tied jigs in a solution of water and *Woolite* overnight, then rinse with cold water, and hang to air dry. This is done to remove any oils on the hair that might prevent absorption of the dye. I boil up a concentrated solution of the dye with a few ounces of white vinegar added. The vinegar is the key to success. I then dump the dye solution into a 1-gallon pickle jar that I save for the occasion. The bucktails are strung together on some leader material and then dunked into the hot dye solution. I swirl the contents of the jar to make sure all of the hair is covered. The jigs are done in a couple of hours, at which point they're rinsed and hung to dry. The jar is then capped to save the dye for future use. The threads and the jig head paint will typically absorb the color of the dye, yielding a uniform-colored result. This dyeing method works very well with most colors, but I've had rather poor results with fluorescent colors.

Getting started at bucktail making requires investing a few dollars for the melter, molds, and tying materials, but if you go through at least a couple of dozen jigs each year, you'll likely be in the black the first season. The flexibility in choosing hook sizes and styles may be the greatest benefit to fluke anglers making their own bucktails. Once you become proficient at it, you'll find there is endless room for experimentation. Colors can be mixed, different materials such as Mylar can be added, heads can be modified, and so on. Besides saving money and enjoying a convenient supply of properly constructed jigs, you'll also get to experience the extra satisfaction of catching fish on your own creations.

Homemade bucktails tied from brown and white hair.

CHAPTER 13
PARTING ADVICE

A *gamefish* is a fish pursued for sport by recreational anglers. Fluke definitely fit that definition, but it's hard not to think of them first as a food fish. Hopefully the preceding chapters and supporting videos will help you put more fluke on the dinner plate. The process of converting the catch to high quality meals should start the moment that you decide to keep a fish.

Keeping fish in good condition for the table is easy if you're in a boat, but can present some challenges if you're walking the beach or are fishing from the limited space of a kayak. As mentioned in the beach fishing chapter, I often cover a lot of ground when I'm fishing the shore. If I want to keep fish, I'll bring a soft cooler bag with a shoulder strap. Mine is a 24- by 20-inch Canyon model B30 Flounder/Fluke/Blackfish Kayak Bag. Canyon makes many different size bags. Another candidate for keeping a few fluke on the beach is the slightly smaller model B32 Steelhead Bait Kayak Bag. These bags work well in combination with frozen gel cold packs.

When I'm kayak fishing, I sometimes keep fish on a stringer in the water. Fluke are pretty hardy and will stay alive for hours this way, even with water temperatures into the 70s. One or two fluke on a stringer don't add much resistance when paddling, so I'll leave them in the water all of the time. If I have more than two fluke on the stringer, I'll take them out of the water while paddling between drifts.

Keeping some species of fish on a stringer can be problematic because the fish might struggle and build up lactic acid, which can degrade the taste. I have not found this to be true with fluke. Maybe

This Canyon cooler bag is a fine mobile option for keeping fish cold on the beach or kayak.

this is because they tend to glide along on the end of the rope and don't thrash around much. My personal experience is that I've never noticed a difference in taste between the fluke I've kept on a stinger and those that went straight to a cooler. However, there's no doubt that the best way to handle fish meant for the table is to put them on ice immediately. If you have sufficient space on your kayak to hold a cooler of fish conveniently while fishing, this is definitely preferable to putting them on a stringer. As the Canyon bag model names imply, these are great cold storage solutions for kayaks. I bring mine when I anticipate a long day on the water. My 24x20-inch model fits behind me in the tank well.

Shark encounters can be a concern in some areas when considering keeping fish in the water on a stringer. My odds of encountering a shark while fluke fishing are very low, but I keep a sharp knife ready to cut the stringer in case of the unexpected. In areas where sharks are a very real possibility, it's probably better to use a cooler instead of a stringer.

If you're boat fishing it's worth the effort to bleed your catch before icing. As soon as a fish that will be kept is landed, make a cut through the gills with a sharp knife and then put the fish head-first into a bucket that's partially filled with water. The fish will bleed out in a few minutes, at which point you can put it in an iced cooler. If you've never done this before, you'll notice the benefit immediately when filleting the fish, as the fillet will be white and blood-free. A kayak angler could bleed fish on a stringer before putting them in a cooler, but this would obviously be a bad idea in any area with sharks.

There are a few different ways to fillet a fluke, and I'll share the way that works best for me. This method results in two fillets for each side of the fish. Begin with the white side up and the fish pointing away from you. Starting at the head, just to the left of the gills, make a lengthwise cut along the center of the fish all the way to the tail. This

Keeping fluke on a stringer while kayak fishing is a good option for a few hours as long as the water is not very warm and sharks aren't a problem.

will give you a starting point to work the knife from the backbone out to the side fins while riding along the skeleton. Now turn the fish around and cut the opposite fillet, backbone to fins. This side has the stomach, so you'll want to stop short of that and avoid puncturing it. It's not a problem if you hit the stomach, but it's best to avoid so that the work area stays cleaner and free of digestive juices. Do the same on the brown side of the fish, but start with it facing toward you. You should now have four fillets. To skin a fillet, push down on the tail end of the fillet to get a firm hold, and work the knife along the inside of the skin. Once you get it started, grip the skin and pull as you run the knife to the head of the fillet. A nice benefit of skinning the fillet is that it will take some of the red meat with it, and this is usually unpleasantly strong tasting.

Fresh fish is unbeatable, but fluke is very well suited for freezing for extended periods if packaged properly. For this I insist on using a *FoodSaver* vacuum sealer. I've served fluke fillets that were frozen for close to a year in vacuum sealed bags without a noticeable difference in taste.

I'm no chef, but I'll share a recipe that's just too good and easy not to pass along. Preheat oil to 375 degrees in a large covered frying pan. I prefer olive oil for this. It's more expensive, but much healthier. While the oil is heating, combine and stir "Complete" pancake mix and water until you have a batter consistency. There are numerous brands that say "Complete" on the box, as only the addition of water is required if you were making pancakes. The amount of pancake mix that you'll need will depend on how many fillets you're coating, but will probably be between one and two cups. Cut the fillets into pieces that you're comfortable with and coat them with the batter. The oil is usually hot by the time I'm done coating. Having an accurate reading of the oil temperature is important. The fillets will soak up the oil and be greasy if it's not hot enough. If you overheat the oil to the point that it starts smoking, about 400 degrees for olive oil, you'll damage the oil which can result in unhealthy byproducts and burnt fillets. An electric deep fryer or the use of a candy thermometer can assure correct temperature. Carefully add the fillets to the hot oil, and flip them after you see they're turning golden brown. This usually takes two or three minutes. After the turned fillets have had another couple of minutes·

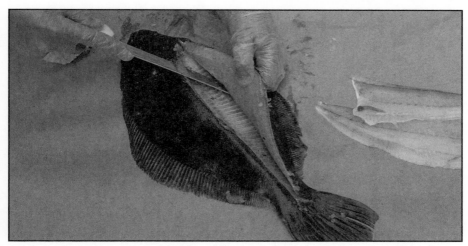

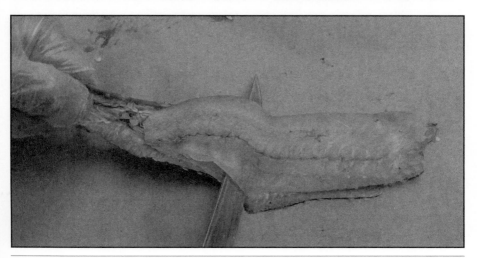

375 degrees is a good oil temperature for frying fish.

in the oil, remove them from the pan and place them on a plate with paper towels to drain. The result is delicious!

Being able to keep fluke for the table legally requires staying on top of regulations that change frequently in some areas. In many regions most of your catch will not be large enough to keep, but a fair percentage will be close to the legal size limit. Be aware that fluke must be measured with the mouth closed. If you lay a fluke down on a measuring device without taking the care to close the mouth, it will probably measure at least a half-inch longer than if it's measured by a conservation officer. That can turn into an expensive mistake if your catch is checked by law enforcement.

If you're serious about fishing, keep a log. Even if you do nothing more than write down some basic information in a notebook that includes, date, location, weather and water conditions, tide, techniques, and catch, you'll be much better off than if you try to keep everything in your head. As my regular readers know, I'm so serious about logging that I wrote a piece of software to make logging and analysis easier. You can learn about that at FishersLog.com. Even if you have no desire to keep an electronic log, the website's screen shots can give a good idea of the important information to record in a notebook.

Strive to use the lightest weight jigs that will stay in the strike zone. The biggest mistake that I see novice anglers make is that they'll use a bucktail that's too heavy for the application. The proper weight jig will glide, dart, and swim in a realistic fashion. A bucktail that's too heavy seeks out the bottom like a rock. A key to being able to use a light-weight jig is to fish with as thin a main line as possible. Braided 15-pound-test line is right in most of the applications in this book, with 20-pound-test used only in deeper settings where a stiffer rod is called for to handle a heavier jig. Finally, make sure all of your jig and teaser hooks are rust-free and have needle-sharp points. It's an often overlooked detail that can make a big difference in your catch.

One of my favorite aspects of fluke fishing is the diverse range of environments in which they can be caught. We spent time in these different settings because having the skills to catch whether you're in the surf, on a sandbar, or drifting over the deeper water of an ocean or sound, allows one to stay productive regardless of water and weather conditions. This is especially important to an angler with limited free time, because when you have time to fish, you probably don't want to spend it away from the water because the wind or waves weren't right.

Learning to catch in the different environments can be challenging in the beginning. The first thirty minutes that I ever spent trying to catch fluke from an ocean beach might have been my last if I wasn't patient or if my expectations were too high. That first half hour on the sand produced nothing but sea robins, but I stayed with it, moved down the shore, and targeted some different structure in the same way that I would have moved my boat or kayak if I wasn't catching while drift fishing. Eventually I found some deeper water within casting distance that held a few fluke. I didn't catch any large enough to keep on that first trip, but I gained some confidence that I was on the right track. I was able to build on that experience and now put together good catches in that area with consistency, including the fish on the cover of this book.

There are many miles of productive shoreline along The Flounder Coast, but some beaches are just plain duds and don't hold many fish. If you're not catching, make moves that change something, such as beach structure, water depth, or current flow. If you're in a general area with fluke, you'll eventually find where they congregate. This might require some research and effort, but figuring things out on your own and discovering a good spot can be one of the most enjoyable aspects of fishing.

It's unlikely you'll ever see a fluke leap from the water with your lure in its mouth, or strip line from your reel so fast that your spool heats up. We save those experiences for other gamefish that don't have both eyes on the same side of their head. The fluke angler's excitement comes from more subtle stimuli – the sharp tap on a bounced jig, the sudden feeling of weight on the end of your line, the unmistakable shake of the rod tip that tells you without a doubt that you've just fooled your dinner. Though not as dramatic, these experiences are no less satisfying. While the ultimate goal might be golden fried and on a dinner plate, making it happen provides the most valuable rewards to those who pursue this special fish.

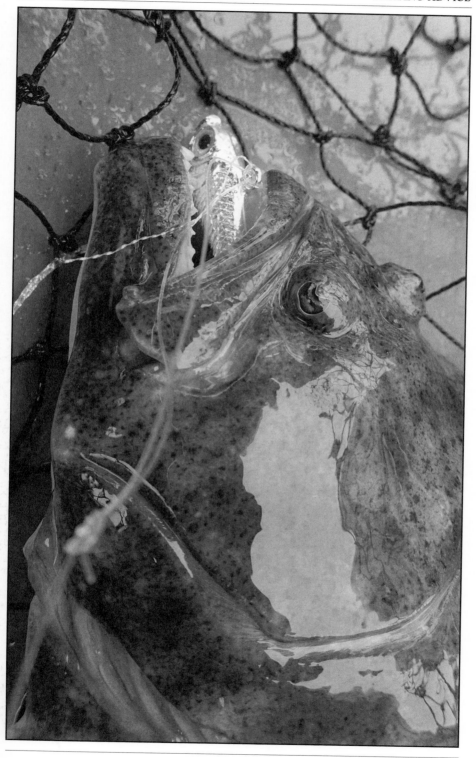

OTHER BOOKS WRITTEN BY
JOHN SKINNER

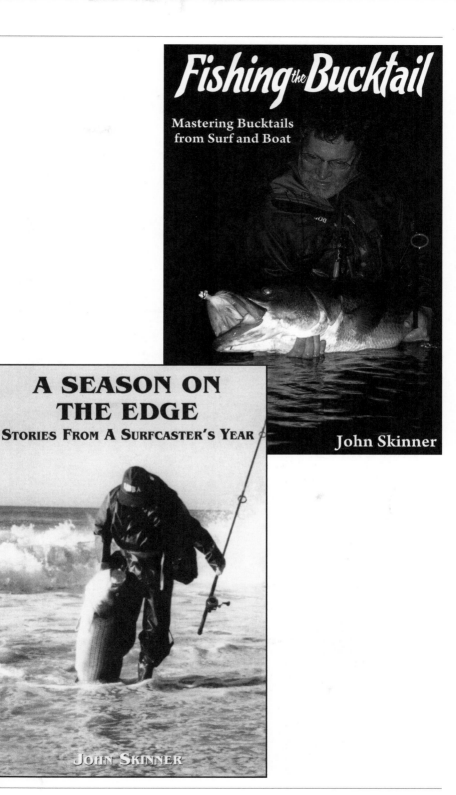